PSYCHOLOGY RE

# SUSTAINABLE EVIDENCE-BASED DECISION-MAKING

# PSYCHOLOGY RESEARCH PROGRESS SERIES

**Suicide and the Creative Arts**
*Steven Stack and David Lester (Editors)*
2009. ISBN: 978-1-60741-958-7

**Suicide and the Creative Arts**
*Steven Stack and David Lester (Editors)*
2009. ISBN: 978-1-60876-560-7 (Online Book)

**Jung Today: Volume 1 - Adulthood**
*Francesco Bisagni  Nadia Fina and Caterina Vezzoli (Editors)*
2009. ISBN: 978-1-60741-893-1

**Jung Today: Volume 2 - Childhood and Adolescence**
*Francesco Bisagni, Nadia Fina and Caterina Vezzoli (Editors)*
2009. ISBN: 978-1-60741-894-8

**Psychological Scientific Perspectives on Out of Body and Near Death Experiences**
*Craig D. Murray (Editor)*
2009. ISBN: 978-1-60741-705-7

**Psychology Research Yearbook, Volume 1**
*Alexandra M. Columbus (Editor)*
2009. ISBN: 978-1-60741-573-2

**Psychology of Burnout: Predictors and Coping Mechanisms**
*Rachel V. Schwartzhoffer (Editor)*
2009. ISBN: 978-1-60876-010-7

**Perchance to Dream: The Frontiers of Dream Psychology**
*Stanley Krippner and  Debbie Joffe Ellis (Editors)*
2009. ISBN: 978-1-60876-123-4

**Stress in the Year 2010 and Beyond**
*Michael F. Shaughnessy (Editor)*
2009. ISBN: 978-1-60876-444-0

**Neuropsychology of the Sense of Agency**
*Michela Balconi*
2010. ISBN: 978-1-60876-358-0

**A Multiple Self Theory of Personality**
*David Lester*
2010. ISBN: 978-1-60876-783-0

**The Psychological Impact of Living Under Violence and Poverty in Brazil**
*Giovanni Marcos Lovisi, Jair de Jesus Mari and Elie S. Valencia (Editors)*
2010. ISBN: 978-1-60876-587-4

**Sustainable Evidence-Based Decision-Making**
*Francesco Chiappelli*
2010. ISBN: 978-1-60876-665-9

PSYCHOLOGY RESEARCH PROGRESS SERIES

# SUSTAINABLE EVIDENCE-BASED DECISION-MAKING

## FRANCESCO CHIAPPELLI

Nova Science Publishers, Inc.
*New York*

### NOTICE TO THE READER
The Publisher has taken reasonable care in the preparation of this book, but makes no expressed or implied warranty of any kind and assumes no responsibility for any errors or omissions. No liability is assumed for incidental or consequential damages in connection with or arising out of information contained in this book. The Publisher shall not be liable for any special, consequential, or exemplary damages resulting, in whole or in part, from the readers' use of, or reliance upon, this material.

Independent verification should be sought for any data, advice or recommendations contained in this book. In addition, no responsibility is assumed by the publisher for any injury and/or damage to persons or property arising from any methods, products, instructions, ideas or otherwise contained in this publication.

This publication is designed to provide accurate and authoritative information with regard to the subject matter covered herein. It is sold with the clear understanding that the Publisher is not engaged in rendering legal or any other professional services. If legal or any other expert assistance is required, the services of a competent person should be sought. FROM A DECLARATION OF PARTICIPANTS JOINTLY ADOPTED BY A COMMITTEE OF THE AMERICAN BAR ASSOCIATION AND A COMMITTEE OF PUBLISHERS.

LIBRARY OF CONGRESS CATALOGING-IN-PUBLICATION DATA

Chiappelli, Francesco.
  Sustainable evidence-based decision-making / Francesco Chiappelli.
    p. cm.
  Includes bibliographical references and index.
  ISBN 978-1-60876-665-9 (hardcover)
  1. Decision making. 2. Sustainable development. I. Title.
  HD30.23.C466 2009
  658.4'032--dc22
                        2009041998

*Published by Nova Science Publishers, Inc. ✦ New York*

# CONTENTS

# PREFACE

In the situation that finds us, the road most traveled is that which we all know best, and which makes us most comfortable. It often is the pathway that brings us to excessive waste, unrecyclable materials and fuels, and arrogant impositions and demands upon communities and surroundings: all in the name of our commodity. We have come to use the word "globalization" to mean in the minds of many imposing of "my way", because "you are still ignorant of the best way (which is my way, of course)": hence, it is my responsibility, duty and intent "to educate you" to my way. Certainly, this is a rash generalization, which we will need to address and rectify in the course of this monograph. It nevertheless shines the light unto why, in many instances, the road most traveled is one of unsustainable behaviors, decisions, and actions in the short and long term. By contrast, the road less traveled, actually the road most often not taken , is that which seeks valid, viable and sustainable solutions for the betterment of the individual, local communities, societies, cultures, regions.

# ABSTRACT[*]

As we enter into the second decade of this century and millennium, it behooves us to ponder whence we came and where the road is leading us. As often happens to travelers, the journey has brought us to a fork in the road, and we must decide whether to take the path on this side or that.

In the situation that finds us, the road most traveled is that which we all know best, and which makes us most comfortable. It often is the pathway that brings us to excessive waste, unrecyclable materials and fuels, and arrogant impositions and demands upon communities and surroundings: all in the name of our commodity. We have come to use the word "globalization" to mean in the minds of many imposing "my way", because "you are still ignorant of the best way (which is my way, of course)": hence, it is my responsibility, duty and intent "to educate you" to my way.

Certainly, this is a rash generalization, which we will need to address and rectify in the course of this monograph. It nevertheless shines the light unto why, in many instances, the road most traveled is one of unsustainable behaviors, decisions, and actions in the short and long term. By contrast, the road less traveled, actually the road most often not taken[1], is that which seeks valid, viable and sustainable solutions for the betterment of the individual,

---

[*] In the words of Philosophy: "...what I look for is not library walls adorned with ivory and glass, but your mind's abode; for I have installed there not books, but what gives books their value, the doctrine found in my writings of old...". Boethius, Consolation of Philosophy, chap 5

1 Two roads diverged in a yellow wood,/And sorry I could not travel both/And be one traveler, long I stood/And looked down one as far as I could/To where it bent in the undergrowth;

Then took the other, as just as fair,/And having perhaps the better claim,/Because it was grassy and wanted wear;/Though as for that the passing there/Had worn them really about the same,

And both that morning equally lay/In leaves no step had trodden black./Oh, I kept the first for another day!/Yet knowing how way leads on to way,/I doubted if I should ever come back.

I shall be telling this with a sigh/Somewhere ages and ages hence:/Two roads diverged in a wood, and I—/I took the one less traveled by,/And that has made all the difference.

The Road Not Taken (1916) by Robert Frost (26 March 1874 – 29 January 1963)

local communities, societies, cultures, regions: the planet, its people as well as its vegetable and animal life forms.

We are called to decide among options and alternatives; and our decisions, if we are to take the road not/less traveled – as hard and arduous as it might be – must be sustainable. In order to make sustainable decisions, we must be empowered to do so by gaining access to the best available evidence. That is to say, in brief, that sustainable decisions must be evidence-based: only that formula will permit us to proffer to the next generations a transformation from the unsustainable, multi-tiered, complex crises that challenge our world today to a sustainable path to recovery. This action calls for an arduous, concerted and sustained effort on the part of many professionals toward a better world.

"yes – we can"[2], and our possibility and potential is grounded in our ability to make sustainable evidence-based decisions. This is the focus of this monograph.

---

2 The empowering force of this simple phrase was amply demonstrated in the election of Pres. B. Obama, Nobel Peace Laureate 2009. May it also drive our societies, and each of us individually toward evidence-based sustainable decisions for the benefit of our and of future generations.

# ABBREVIATIONS

| Acronym | Term | Definition (if applicable) |
|---|---|---|
| AASHE | Association for the Advancement of Sustainability in Higher Education | |
| ACUPCC | American College & University Presidents Climate Commitment | |
| ADA | American Dental Association | |
| AHP | Analytic Hierarchy Process | a multi-criteria evaluation and decision support system |
| AMSTAR | assessment of multiple systematic reviews | |
| CER | Comparative Effectiveness Research | |
| CT | Communication Technology | |
| DLT | Dose Limiting Toxicity | |
| DoE | Department of Energy | |
| DWH | Distributed Data Warehouses | |
| EBD | Evidence-Based Decisions | |
| EBPo | Evidence-based Policy | |
| EBPr | Evidence-Based Practice | |
| EBR | Evidence-Based Research | |
| EPC | Environment Performance Criteria | |
| FDA | Food and Drug Administration | |
| GhG | Greenhouse Gas | |
| GIS | Geographic Information Systems | integration of hardware, software, and data for capturing, managing, analyzing, and displaying all forms of geographically referenced information. It allows to view, understand, question, interpret, and visualize data in many ways |

| | | |
|---|---|---|
| | | that reveal relationships, patterns, and trends in the form of maps, globes, reports, and charts. |
| GRADE | Grading of Recommendations Assessment, Development and Evaluation | The GRADE approach to grading the quality of evidence and strength of recommendations provides a comprehensive and transparent approach for developing clinical recommendations about using diagnostic tests or diagnostic strategies |
| HEASC | Higher Education Associations Sustainability Consortium | |
| IND | Investigational New Drug | |
| IT – HIT | Information Technology - Human Information technology | |
| LEED | Leadership in Energy and Environmental Design | |
| MCDA | Multicriteria Decision Analysis | |
| MeSH | medical subject heading | |
| MTD | Maximum Tolerated Dose | |
| P-GIS | Participatory GIS | P-GIS offers tools that can be used to help the public become meaningfully involved in decision-making processes affecting their communities. |
| QoL | Quality of Life | |
| R-AMSTAR | revised AMSTAR | |
| rCPG's | revised common & practical guidelines | |
| RS | Research Synthesis | |
| SD | Starting Dose | |
| SoL | Standard of Living | |
| SOP | Standard Operating Procedure | |
| STARS | Sustainability Tracking, Assessment, and Rating System | |
| UCS | Union of Concerned Scientists | |
| UCSAN | Union of Concerned Scientists Action Network | |
| USGBC | United States Green Building Council | |
| ZeV | Zero-emission Vehicle | |

# Chapter 1

# INTRODUCTION

"…what information consumes is rather obvious: it consumes the attention of its recipients. Hence a wealth of information creates a poverty of attention, and a need to allocate that attention efficiently among the overabundance of information sources that might consume it…" (Herber Alexander Simon, 1971)

The process of sustainable decision-making from this vantage point[3] - i.e., of consumption of certain exhaustible resources – is a process of informed choice among the probability distributions for each event or occurrence. It is not concerned with defining objectives, designing the alternatives or assessing the consequences, except to the extent that those are either given from outside or previously determined. Rather, it becomes a mere process of ranking based on a choice criterion subjective to, driven by, and determined by the decision maker's objectives and preferences for improving the quality of life (QoL) and standard of living (SoL) of all the members of a community, locally and globally[4]. Given a set of alternatives, a set of consequences, and a correspondence between those sets, decision theory offers conceptually simple procedures for choice and process, the realization of which is often intricate, complex and debatable.

Under conditions of certainty, the decision maker's objectives and preferences are simulated by a single-attribute that establishes the ranking criteria. By

---

3 The prospect view of decision-making, for instance, proposes that each subjective value is modeled by a value function that is concave for gains, convex for losses, and steeper for losses than for gains. Probabilities for outcomes lean onto a weighting function that overweights low probabilities and underweights moderate to high probabilities, and which can be traced to certain neuroscience pathways (cf., the cognitive neuroscience of decision making) (vide infra) (Trepel et al, 2005; Tom et al, 2007).

4 hence., "sustainable" decisions, vide infra

contrast, under the more realistic conditions of risk and overlapping realities and perceptions, the concept of utility[5] is introduced. Preferences and objectives must have mutually exclusive consequences, for the utility alternative to be described and quantified by a utility function, which renders the expected utility for each alternative. The alternative with the highest expected utility weighs heavier in the sustainable decision-making process, and is considered by some to be the most preferable.

For instance, under common occurrences of uncertainty, sustainable decisions may utilize standard criteria of choice, such as those utilized in gambling and betting, where the chosen alternative is that which produces the worst possible consequence that is still better than, or at least equal to the best possible consequence of any other alternative. Alternatively, when the uncertainty can be reduced to the case of risk by using subjective probabilities, then the more reliable utility approach noted above can be used.

The human mind and human cognitive abilities are limited. This very inherent limitation in our intellectual schemata limits the decision-maker by erecting "filters" (Kerckhoff & Davis, 1962) through which evidence and facts are screened, diluted, exacerbated, and evaluated[6]. Further, another limitation to our decision-making ability lies in capturing the relevant evidence to generate a coherent whole that will eventually engender another fundamental bias in the process of making decisions. These effects result in explanatory coherence that is the simpler, the easier to understand, the faster to capture, the more likely a given hypothesis, thesis or decision will be acceptable and accepted (Thagard, 1989). A corollary of this occurs when the decision-maker is facing a choice between familiar[7] vs. novel, or appropriate vs. distinct, facts and bits of evidence. According to the law of Perceptual Contrast Effects[8] (Sherif et al, 1958), decision-

---

5 Utility generally refers to the precise degree of personal satisfaction, pleasure, or sense of want-fulfillment derived from the outcome of a given decision. Evidently, no two decision-makers assign identical utilities to any given outcome or set of outcomes, because individual differences in preferences, values and priorities. But, presumably, some rough standard to compare utilities of various possible decision outcomes is possible, if the construct of utility is a measurable and quantifiable entity – a sine qua non to the principle of diminishing marginal utility. This is particularly relevant to the domain of sustainability, as discussed in Part III below.

6 For example emotional filters, socio-cultural filters, acculturation filters, attributional filters, motivational filters, personal preference filter, and the like.

7 the Mere Exposure Theory in cognitive psychology proposes that the more exposure we have to a stimulus, fact or evidence, the more we will tend to accept it as true, as standard, and as the optimal choice. Familiarity breeds liking more than contempt, and thus acts powerfully in the decision-making process (Kunst-Williams and Zajonc, 1980; Sawyer, 1981).

8 Somewhat related to Thorndike' Halo Effect: When we consider a piece of evidence good or bad (i.e., useful or not in a give decision-making process) in one given criterion, we are likely to extent a similar evaluation for other criteria (Thorndike, 1920).

makers tend to favor comparing the novel vs. the familiar, and the dissimilar vs. the similar[9].

This monograph discusses how this and other perspectives are applied to the process of making sustainable decisions.

---

9 Of course, the situation increases in complexity as the number of options increase. Compensatory strategies focus on similarities, and permit to trade off attributes of similar priority, whereas non-compensatory strategies stress differences in attributes (Payne, 1982).

*Chapter 2*

# THE PROCESS OF DECISION-MAKING[10]

## 2.1. FUNDAMENTALS OF DECISION THEORY

Decision[11] is a meta-construct. It is often the case that decisions, including sustainable decisions, are to be made without advance knowledge of their consequences.

Decision theory consists of the body of social and cognitive psychology, constructs of knowledge and related analytical techniques of different degrees of formality, and can be viewed to emerge from probability theory that it can apply to conditions of certainty, risk[12], or uncertainty[13], where the probability of occurrence for each consequence is quantifiable. Risk is distinct from uncertainty in that, risk, but not uncertainty *per se*, has options that are well specified or

---

10 This section is elaborated from the chapter Chiappelli et al. in Chiappelli et al, Eds. Understanding Evidence-Based Practice: Toward Optimizing Clinical Outcomes. Springer (2009), and in Chiappelli F, Cajulis OS. The logic model in evidence-based clinical decision-making in dental practice. J Evid Based Dent Pract 2009 (In Press).

11 from Latin dēcīsĭo, decisionis, noun, f; dēcīdo, dēcīdis, decidi, decisum, dēcīdĕre, verb

12 The term "risk" in the context of this discussion means "uncertainty" for which the probability distribution is known. Risk analysis pertains to the statistical evaluation of the outcomes of decisions along with their probabilities.

13 In the context of probability and decision theory, the term "uncertainty", by contrast, pertains to a measure of variety. When uncertainty is null (H=0), it implies no variety among the elements of the set: they are all the same, and known to be the same. As uncertainty increases, H increases, both as a function of the number of elements in the set, and their equi-probability. The uncertainty among multiple sets is summative (H1+H2+...Hn=Ht). Nonetheless, the measure of uncertainty, H, remains a relative weak quantification because it is subjective: since the elements in a given set are usually specified by the observer, the uncertainty of the set has inherent variance deriving from individual differences among observers. Uncertainty variance can be minimized by randomization, stratification and other statistical techniques.

transparent outcomes with certain probabilities of occurrence attached to them (Trepel et al, 2005; Tom et al, 2007). Alternatives of occurrence are associated with a probability distribution.

Decision-making principles are designed to guide the decision-maker in choosing among alternatives in light of their possible consequences. The process of making decisions is grounded on knowledge and expertise, and is driven by fundamental, ethical, cultural, psycho-emotional and biological principles. It reflects the psycho-emotional inner world of perception of the decision-maker, and rests on fundamentals of socio-economic principles and realities.

Most of decision evaluation is either normative or prescriptive. It aims at identifying the best decision, assuming that the decision maker is fully and properly informed, able to rationalize, and fully capable of inductive[14] and deductive reasoning. The practical application of prescriptive decision-making approach is known as decision analysis. It consists in providing decision support systems, in the form of the best available evidence, tools, methodologies and software to help people make the best possible decisions for the betterment of society.

One important contribution of decision analysis is that it reveals that, in most instances, the decision-making process suffers from inherent bias. In this context, bias tends to behave as the augmenting or the discounting principles[15]. Bias in decision-making are principally consequential to the construct of "bounded rationality", which, as eloquently discussed by Herbert Simon[16] close to three

---

14 inductive reasoning (i.e., , inductive logic) proposes that the premises of an argument support the conclusion, without ensuring its absolute truth. It allows generalizations based on individual observations, and serves to ascribe properties or to describe relations to sets based on observational events. It can be used to formulate hypotheses or laws based on limited observations of recurring phenomenal patterns. Deductive reasoning, by contrast, moves from given premises (all health care interventions must strive toward sustainable solutions: major premise; dentistry is a form of health care intervention: minor premise) to a conclusion (dentistry must strive toward sustainable solutions: conclusion), which cannot be untrue if the premises are true.

15 Each added piece of evidence adds toward –augments – or detracts from – discounts – the probability of making a decision. This process is following principles very much akin to basic Bayesian statistics. Anticipated new evidence contributes to this probability in an expected manner, but, unexpected new evidence carries the risk of a disproportionate positive (i.e., "augmenting") or negative (i.e., "discounting") incremental effect.

16 Herbert A. Simon (15 June 1916 – 9 February 2001), political scientist, cognitive psychologist, academician at Carnegie Mellon Univ. Nobel Laureate in Economics, 1978. In his doctoral dissertation (Administrative Behavior: A Study of Decision-Making Processes in Administrative Organizations, 1947), he laid the foundations of his life-long academic discourse on the behavioral and the cognitive processes of making rational human choices. Simon proposes that decisions can range from the listing of evidence and alternatives, to probability of consequences, to the assessment and comparison of the accuracy and efficiency of each of these sets of

decades ago, states that decision-makers have a limited time and availability to make decisions, and are limited by cognitive schemata and by other decisional limitations, such as the availability of evidence[17] (Simon, 1982).

Several decision-making theories can be articulated along two main families, which are briefly introduced below in the context of making sustainable decisions. Somatic states, such as emotions and circuits within our nervous system[18], can play a powerful role in the process of making decisions, and can be described by their neuroanatomical and neurophysiological substrata[19]. The brain employs multiple levels of neuronal processing when it is engaged in the functions that lead to making decisions. This view supports our current understanding of dual-processing theories, which argue for the dissociation between automatic and controlled components of processing.

Behavioral output data – that is, observations of behaviors, and behavioral experiments - show beyond doubt that the brain is capable of dual processing. We can, and we do, distinguish consciously or subconsciously, between automatic and controlled processing in our judgment- and decision-making. However, our knowledge of fundamental neuroscience has not, to this date, elucidated if, and how this automatic vs. controlled processing dichotomy corresponds to specific neural substrate[20] (Sanfey & Chang, 2008).

---

consequences. The correctness of decisions, he argues, is measured by 1) the adequacy of achieving the desired objective, and 2) the efficiency with which the result was obtained. Decisions, he argues, are complex admixture of facts and values.

17 Vide infra, sustainable decisions based on the evidence vs evidence-based sustainable decisions.

18 All processes in the brain, including learning, memory, perceptions, emotions, motivations, and all aspects of what we call "cognition" are processes by neurons. Neurons are specialized cells that process and transmit information by electrochemical signaling, and are the core components of the brain, and the peripheral nerves. Their activity in the brain is modulated by other cells (e.g., astrocytes, oligodendrocytes, microglia), and by inter-neurons that connect neurons to other neurons, and permit the exquisitely complex pattern, and potential of responses. Neuroscientists speak of neural network to describe a population of physically interconnected neurons, or a group of disparate neurons whose inputs or signalling targets together define a recognizable circuit. Neuronal circuits are distinct functional entities of interconnected neurons that are capable of influencing each other, and modulating each other's firing responses (Muller & Insua, 1995). A system exists in humans that is involved in predicting rewards, and thus guides behavior, including the making and the acting upon decisions. The system involves a circuit including the striatum, the orbito-frontal cortex and the amygdala, and is accentuated and incentivized by "a mentalizing system" and a reward system, which by current sophisticated imaging techniques, can be localized to the medial prefrontal cortex, in particular the anterior paracingulate cortex (Walter et al, 2005).

19 which in turn become the "inducers" of the decision-making process (Damasio et al, 1991).

20 Since the dorsolateral prefrontal cortex, for example, plays such an important role in cognitive representations in working memory, it might also play a role in decision-making by representing prospects (vide infra) and subsequent decision utility computations.

One very important tool in research of the neural substrata of decision-making is neuroimaging[21]. To date, this technique has used classic moral dilemmas to identify the neural circuitry involved in moral decision-making in normal men and women. A challenging question is how this circuit functions in immoral, psychopathic individuals[22], as a possible key to understanding ill-fated or bad decisions, and grossly unsustainable decisions[23]. Ongoing studies suggest that individuals with psychopathic personality disorder show reduced activity in the amygdala during emotional moral decision-making. Manipulative individuals manifest significantly reduced activity in the entire moral neural circuit, suggesting that personality disorders and pathologies related to psychopathic behaviors[24] may be associated with certain identifiable deficits in brain regions essential to normal individuals when engaged in making moral judgment and decisions, and consequentially a failure to integrate emotion into decision-making (Glenn et al, 2009).

Our "temperament[25]" may also drive our inclinations to make certain decisions under certain constraints. And the same may be said of the modulation of our decision-making abilities at the higher stages of moral development[26].

---

21 Neuroimaging is a relatively new technique that obtains either directly or indirectly image the structure, function/pharmacology of the brain. There are two principal applications of this protocol: a) structural imaging provides new insights on the structure of the brain in health and disease; and b) functional imaging serves to diagnose metabolic diseases (e.g., Alzheimer's disease), lesions or tumors, and to reveal fundamental functioning of the brain in cognition (e.g., Human Cognonome Project [aimed to reverse engineer the human brain], processing of information, motivation, emotion, sleep, etc.)

22 The conceptualization of psychopathy as a pathological state emerged from The Unscrupulous Man, a work authored by Theophrastus (cca 371 BC – 270 BC), a student of Aristotle, as part of his opera magna on The Characters. In modern psychiatry, the key to its diagnosis, as recommended by the American Psychiatric Association, is a pervasive pattern of disregard for, and violation of, the rights of others that begins in childhood or early adolescence and continues into adulthood.

23 From a purely philosophical perspective, if one considers that sustainable decisions are those which strive to the betterment of the individual and the community, both locally and globally, both for the moment present and for future generations, and if one considers the definition of psychopathy given above, then one would logically infer that unsustainable actions are in se psychopathic in nature, that unsustainable behaviors are as anti-social as psychopathic behaviors are, and that an unsustainable choice of action is as devoid of moral judgment as one arising from a psychopathic tendency.

24 Psychopathy is a personality disorder that involves severe disruption in moral behavior and pronounced deficits in emotion, itself a critical component of moral behavior. Emotion-driven decision-making elicited by moral dilemmas evoke, under experimental conditions, significant activity in the amygdala, medial prefrontal cortex, posterior cingulate and angular gyrus, by functional neuroimaging.

25 The concept of temperaments is very old in biomedicine (cf., Galen or Pergamene, 129-216 AD), but by no means antiquated. In brief, a person who is sanguine is generally spontaneous, light-hearted, and self-confident. A fun-loving people person, who loves to entertain, BUT who can

## 2.2. RATIONAL VS. LOGICAL DECISION-MAKING

Rational decision-making refers to cognitive theory, and postulates that rational human beings make choices between options based on logical choices[27]. Sustainable decisions are not unique in that rational behavior, reasoning, cognitive processes require considerable conscious or subconscious evaluation: as one can assess the rationality of individual choices, so can the rationality of social choices be examined and evaluated to determine the extent to which they are driven by, and related to conscious or subconscious volitions[28], preferences, biased judgments.

Rationality is as central a concept in branches of philosophy such as action theory, epistemology, ethics, and the philosophy of the mind, as it is to the field of

---

also be impulsive, dreamers, detached from reality, bossy, over-confident, arrogant, cocky, and over-indulgent. Such a person manifests typically collaborating behavior. A person who is melancholic is generally thoughtful, creative, kind & considerate, BUT who can also be overly pessimistic, self-focused, depressed, critical and perfectionist. A person with this predominant temperament most often displays avoidance behavior. A person who is choleric is generally driven, ambitious, energetic, passionate, persuasive, BUT who can also be bad-tempered, violent, domineering, abusive. They show competing and often abusive behavior. A person who is phlegmatic is generally calm, cool, settled, grounded, dedicated and faithful, BUT can also be cold, detached, lazy, unadaptable, shy, distant, and unfriendly. This person typically shows compromising behavior. It is now generally accepted that individuals usually show a blend of temperaments, which can vary with the situation, the period of life & development, and social surroundings & influences (cf., Chiappelli et al, 2005).

26 e.g., Erikson's s theory of moral development: e.g., identity & role definition in adolescence, commitment, work ethics and collaboration in young adulthood, generativity vs. intellectual stagnation in mature adulthood, and contemplation of life accomplishment vs. despair in aging.

27 This is quite in contrast to some early behavioristic observations, such as "...human behavior, in general ... is not under the constant and detailed guidance of careful and accurate hedonic calculations, but is the product of an unstable and unrational complex of reflex actions, impulses, instincts, habits, customs, fashion, and hysteria..." (Viner, 1925).

28 progress in neuroscience now allows scientists to trace and characterize the brain circuits and brain areas responsible for volitions, choices, decisions, and all sorts of other behaviors. With respect to conscious and subconscious decisions, for example, research has now identified central nervous system networks that include the pre-supplementary motor area, the anterior prefrontal cortex and the parietal cortex, which together underlie voluntary action: that is, volitions, which are defined as the distinctive conscious experience of intending to act. These brain areas not only control volitions, but also the actual actions toward actualizing these volitions. Volitions, per se, are defined by neuroscientists as a series of decisions, driven consciously or subconsciously, about the necessity to act, when to act, and the manner in which to act (i.e., what action to perform, when to perform it, how to perform it) (Haggard, 2008). It is important to note, however, key limitations of neuroscience protocols of neuroimaging(vide supra) in this context: a) they are expensive, and b) they only determine that different regions of our brain are activated, or not, when the subject is in certain situations, but fail to provide an explanatory substratum (i.e., causality, cause-effect) for the response (i.e., cost/benefit ratios would be prohibitively high in making the decision of whether or not to use neuroimaging); that is to say, unsatisfactory comparative effectiveness – vedi infra, Part II).

decision-making. A *sine qua non* of a rational argument is that it be logically valid. But rationality *per se* is broader than logic because it includes "uncertain but sensible" arguments based on probability expectations and personal experience. Logic only concerns itself with directly provable facts and consequential valid relations among them.

This distinction is particularly important in the domain of sustainable decision-making, because decisions[29] are often taken based on *ad hominem*[30] basis[31], rather than unshakeable logic. Whereas *ad hominem* grounds for decision-making may be logically unsound[32], they are in many cases rational, sensible and practical.

Rationality and reason are essentially similar with respect to the fundamental methods used to analyze experiences, and even, to some extent at least, data gathered through systematically gathered observations and experiments. All that is needed is that the fundamental precept of sustainable rationality is followed, which states that a good rationale must be independent of emotions, personal feelings or instincts.

What is required for an action to be rational is that if one guesses (heuristic, trial-error), believes or knows (based on previous experience[33]) that action X, which can be done (e.g., cook a sausage) implies Y (e.g., not be hungry anymore), and that Y is desirable, then the decision follows to act on X[34]. Such arguments are logically valid but not necessarily logically sound.

This groundwork allowed the work of Max Weber[35] (1864 – 1920) to flourish into an interpretation of decisions for social action (i.e., social decision-making theory) that identifies four distinct levels, or types of rationality:

---

29 as critical to the QoL and the SoL of individuals within the local and the global community, and as important to our generations and our children's – that is decisions as crucial as those that pertain to sustainability of our world, of our planet...

30 an ad hominem argument is generally one that consists of criticizing the person who presents the argument in an attempt to discredit the argument, often for want of substantial faults with the argument itself.

31 Because, most often, ad hominem arguments are used in replying to factual claims or propositions by attacking or appealing to a characteristic or belief of the source or origin of the proposition or claim, rather than by addressing the substance of the argument and producing evidence for or against the claim following the rules of logic.

32 Arguments may well be logically valid, but they may also be unsound, based on the strict rules of logic – which is why, often times, decisions may be rational but appear "illogical"

33 Cf., the Bayesian view on decision-making

34 ...or to avoid X, if the outcome Y is undesirable

35 Weber's work has found proponents as well as critics, including, in the most proximal decades, Habermasian, Eagleton, and Etzioni. The latter reframed the decision-making process and proposed that purposive/instrumental rationality is actually subordinated by normative ideas on

1. **Zweckrational**, the purposeful and instrumental type of rational behavior that characterizes the expectations about the behavior of others in a social environment. Rational expectations lead to decisions, which Weber himself described as "rationally pursued and calculated."

2. **Wertrational**, the rational behavior that is oriented toward a set of values, or belief system, and that leads to decisions that favor ethical, aesthetic, religious or other motives, independent of the expected success, the logic behind it, or the social benefit (cf., fanaticism)

3. **affect-driven** rational behavior, which Weber conceptualized as being determined by the actor's emotions, affect, and feelings, or emotion, which may be akin to the subconscious volitions discussed above).

4. **traditions and habituation**: ingrained behaviors.

From there, and with slight semantic modifications, arose the current rational choice theory, which has become the contemporary theoretical model framework of choice for understanding and formally modeling social and economic behavior and decision-making in social and socio-political domain, and a sustainable environment. Several models of rational choice exist, but all converge on the fundamental tenet that individuals choose and decide upon the best action according to, and based upon the set of preferences, psycho-cognitive functions, and socio-environmental constraints facing them[36]. Models differ for the additional assumptions they propose, although it widely recognized that none provide a full and complete description of reality: they simply allow the generation of testable working hypotheses, which must then undergo empirical tests.

This theoretical paradigm was severely challenged by Green and Shapiro for the prohibitive limitations in empirical outputs that rational choice theory can generate, particularly in the domain of political and social science (Green and Shapiro, 1994). Schram and Caterino (2006) have also presented in depth fundamental methodological criticism of rational choice theory for not permitting methodological pluralism.

---

how people 'ought' to behave and affective considerations of how people "wish" to behave (Etzioni , 1988).

36 In brief, rational choice theory argues that patterns of behavior in societies reflect the choices made by individuals as they seek to maximize benefits and minimize costs. In this light, decision-making depends primarily and rationally from comparing costs and benefits of different courses of action, and patterns of individual and social behavior develop and become established solely as a result of those choices (cf., comparative effectiveness research, vide infra, Part II)

Being that as it may, it remains a useful conceptualization of decision-making theory. This is particularly so in the context of sustainability and sustainable evidence-based decisions, as we show below.

The logic model[37], by contrast to the above, proffers a general cognitive framework for describing the fundamental rational and logic process of decision-making that an individual, a group or an organization may follow. The logic model is likely to continue to establish itself as probably the most appropriate in this context for the inherent constraints of the process of sustainable decision-making, as it recently has in the domain of evidence-based decisions (*vide infra*) (Chiappelli & Cajulis, 2009).

In brief, the logic model presents decision-making into four distinct categories, which logically flow into each other and from each other:

1. *inputs* represent materials, data, evidence and other resources such as money, employees, and equipment – inputs lead to
2. *activities*, programs or processes, which in turn derive into
3. *immediate outputs*, products and results of the activities above, which in the short term are to be generated, produced or delivered. The evaluation of the immediacy of these outcomes logically leads to a process of normative and summative evaluation of
4. *long-term consequences* of the outputs, including revised policies.

The strength of the logic model lies in the fact that, for any given decision-making process, working hypotheses can be clearly stated at each step, tested and verified by means of quantifiable, reliable and valid performance measures. Normative and summative evaluation can be obtained at key capstone time-points in order to ensure steady progress toward obtaining anticipated outputs, and desired outcomes, and, in the final analysis, providing justification for testing the model experimentally in any given situation in the first place. The validity and the value of the logic model in sustainable evidence-based decision-making are further elaborated below (cf., Parts II & III).

---

37 The logic model was first proposed by Dr. Joseph Whooley in the late 1970's as an "evaluability assessment", and subsequently refined by others. Dr. Whooley is presently Professor of Public Administration at the University of Southern California and Senior Advisor for Evaluation Methodology in the U.S. General Accounting Office.

## 2.3. DECISIONS BASED ON PROBABILITIES

We opened this section by stating that most decisions are made within a context of absolute or quasi uncertainty for the outcome. To the point, therefore, the generality espoused by the rational theory of decision-making may not always be verified, particularly when, as it often occurs in the realm of sustainability, decisions are made under the prospect of risk and uncertainty[38]. In these instances, an alternate model of decision-making, based seeking to maximize benefit and minimizing cost or risk (cf., utility theory), is employed. This may be an approach of choice in sustainable decisions, when they consider and contrast the relative effectiveness[39] of protocols, instruments or policies.

From a general viewpoint, and as noted above, the term utility[40] refers a measure of perceived or real benefit, relative satisfaction from, or desirability of, for example, in the context of sustainability, increase in quality of life (QoL)[41] and standard of living (SoL)[42] – as a direct consequence of the utilization of goods or services, such as health care intervention, societal improvements (e.g., urban planning, ergonomics, sustainable architecture), and environmental quality (e.g., pollution, clean energy). It follows that certain interventions, or modifications thereof may contribute to increasing or decreasing such benefits, and therefore the

---

38 contemporary theories in the realm of economics, for instance, conceive homo economicus as a rational decision-maker capable of maximizing utility. In reality, however, people tend to approximate optimal decision-making strategies through a collection of heuristic routines, which may be driven by emotions and/or rectified progressively through learning and experience. Specialized cognitive processes may develop and become imprinted early in development for social decision-making, and, might share their origins and neural mechanisms with the ability to simulate, imagine or recall outcomes expected from alternative actions that an individual can take.

39 i.e., comparative effectiveness research (CER), the science of direct comparison of existing interventions – usually health care-related, although the approach now extends to most, if not all professions - to determine which works best and is most cost-effective with the greatest overall benefits and the least potential harms and risks (Chiappelli et al, 2009) (vide infra).

40 Note the fundamental assumptions that a) the utilities and probabilities of one alternative (or a new alternative) should not influence another alternative; b) alternatives are "transitive": that is they are subject to ordering based on preferences; and c) by the very nature of the process, creativity and any form of cognitive input is excluded, as it rests on probabilistic rules. This is particularly problematic when cases of cognitive dissonance arise (i.e., conflict between the outcome of the probabilistic process and the subject's knowledge, information processing, beliefs or preferences).

41 Quality of life (QoL) is a critical outcome in sustainable decision-making, because of the very nature of sustainability as the science that seeks to ensure the well-being of the individual within the community locally and globally.

42 In the realm of sustainable decisions, SoL is generally rendered as real, inflation adjusted income per person, poverty rate, access and quality of health care, income growth inequality, educational standards, and other similar measures.

utility of said goods or services. That is to say, in simpler and more terms, direct sustainable decision-making can be driven by, and carried out for the purpose of altering utility outcomes.

Utility theory arises from the philosophical tradition of utilitarianism[43], and utility-based decision-making then rest on a rationale centered upon utility-maximizing behavior, more often than driven by economic constraints[44]. More often than not, one essential concern of utility-determined decisions pertain to cost: that is, cost-to-benefit ratio[45] - hence, the relevance to comparative effectiveness research (CER)[46]. That is the principal reason why utility theory of decision-making commonly addresses, and seeks to explain economic behavior.

The concept of cardinal utility refers to the magnitude of utility differences, as an ethically or behaviorally relevant and quantifiable measure[47]. Ordinal utility describes utility rankings, but does not quantify the strength of preferences or benefits. From this viewpoint, utility is best described by the indifference curve,

---

43 Utilitarism proposes that the moral worth of an action is determined by its utility, defined as the potential of its outcome to contributing to happiness or pleasure (or, as Peter Singer [1946 - ] defines it, satisfaction of preferences) of the individual and of society. Finding its origins in the thought of the Greek philosopher Epicurus (341 BC – 270 BC), but developed as a modern form of consequentialism (i.e., the moral worth of an action is determined by its outcome - the ends justify the means when the good, happiness or pleasure versus suffering or pain) are maximized through the work of Jeremy Bentham (1748-1832), John Stuart Mill (1806-1876), and more recently John Rawls (1921-2002). Utilitarism has been criticized as simplistic philosophy of life centered on placing happiness or pleasure as the ultimate importance, goal and purpose of all human endeavors, moral criterion for the organization of society.

44 since – without any philosophical or societal moral judgment of the following statement – happiness, quality of life and, generally speaking, satisfaction of individuals in contemporary society is consequential largely to economic well-being and stability (i.e., "contentment").

45 of course, another critical issue of utility decisions concerns risk/benefit.

46 Vide supra

47 Hence has a branch of utility theory developed that is based on probabilities. Expected utility theory deals with the analysis of choices among risky projects with (possibly multidimensional) outcomes. It was first proposed by Nicholas Bernoulli in 1713 and solved by Daniel Bernoulli in 1738 as the St. Petersburg paradox. This paradox is related both to probability and to decision theory. In brief, it arises from a theoretical lottery game that generates a random variable with infinite expected value (i.e. infinite expected payoff), but that is worth only a small investment of money. The paradox exemplifies the common situation where a naïve decision criterion, which solely considers the expected winning, plays the primary role in directing the course of action that no (sensible rational) person would otherwise take. Daniel Bernoulli (1700-1782) argued that the paradox could be resolved if decision-makers displayed risk aversion and argued for a logarithmic cardinal utility function: that is to say, when marginal utility and finite resources are incorporated in the model, then the paradox resolves. John von Neumann (1903 – 1957) and Oskar Morgenstern (1902 – 1977) used expected utility theory seeking a probability-based maximization in their formulation of game theory. The neural basis of game theory was recently characterized, and the unique features of social decision-making were localized and described in the functions of brain areas involved in reward evaluation and reinforcement learning (Lee, 2008)

which plots the combination of commodities that an individual or a society can accept to maintain a given level of satisfaction[48]. In that respect, individual utility (or societal utility) is expressed as the dependent variable of functions of, for instance, production or commodity. One classic example is the well-known Pareto[49] efficiency curve, which today is a central concept of welfare economics.

Despite the strengths of utility theory in the context of sustainable decision-making, critics have argued that general utilitarian statements across individuals in a social group can actually not be made because different value systems have different perspectives on the use of utility in making moral judgments. In the complexity of today's political reality, for instance, large philosophical and ideological divides exist between Marxist-based regimes, which are subsumed under the general rubric of idealist political systems based Kantian philosophical thought, and more libertarian societies. Whereas they may share the common drive toward the happiness and well being of single individuals, the moral standards of utility and the decisions made to improve and sustain quality of life are fundamentally different across those extremes, and most socio-political systems.

That is why, in fact generally speaking, neither cardinal nor ordinary utility are empirically observable in the real world. Indeed, it is unclear how, in the context of cardinal utility, one can quantify the level of individual or societal satisfaction (i.e., QoL or SoL).

What is clear is that the concept of sustainability, that is the societal drive to improve livelihood of its members, varies across cultures and political systems. The fact remains that the process of sustainable decision-making is impervious to such alien forces, whether it rests on logic or on cost-effective concerns.

As an alternative to expected utility theory[50], Daniel Kahneman (1943 - ) and Amos Tversky (1937 – 1996) proposed Prospect theory in 1979. This theoretical

---

48 The relevance of this model to the themes addressed by sustainability becomes now self-evident.

49 Vilfredo Federico Damaso Pareto (15 July 1848 – 19 August 1923), the Italian economist who helped transform the field of economics from a distant branch of social philosophy into a scientific endeavor. He proposed that given a set of alternative distribution of goods or income to group of individuals, decisions pertaining to changing from one allocation to another can have significant consequences in making one of more individuals in that group better off, without making any other individual worse off. This is the Pareto improvement principle, from which derives the proposition that any given allocation is Pareto efficient (= Pareto optimal) when no further Pareto improvements is achievable. This condition is referred to as a "strong Pareto optimum". The implications of Pareto's thought to sustainability are widespread.

50 Prospect theory rests on empirical evidence - the best available empirical evidence, and in that sense prospect theory is the prototype of evidence-based decision-making -, and seeks to describe how individuals evaluate potential losses and gains, and make choices in situations where they have to decide between alternatives that involve a known or anticipated risk.

model, which actually served to open this discussion, describes the process of making decisions between alternatives that involve risk. While prospect theory alludes to the fact that humans use emotions in decision-making, it in fact fails to use explicitly the term 'emotions'. Rather, the theory attributes our lapse in rational thinking when making decisions to some other unexplained factor. As a real-life and descriptive model, it utilizes concrete choices, rather than optimal hypothetical situations and decisions. It is grounded on the reality of life events and situations, and considers alternatives with uncertain outcomes, where the probabilities are known, and therefore also important options for sustainable decision-making.

In conclusion, it is important to state that the field of decision-making is vast, complex and firmly anchored in a long tradition. Banning (2007) summarized it well:

> "...(sustainable) decision making is a unique process that involves the interplay between knowledge of pre-existing... conditions, explicit ... information, ... and experiential learning. Historically, two models of ... decision making are recognized from the '/literature; the information-processing model and the intuitive-humanist model...the information-procession model is rooted in ... decision making... (and) ...uses a scientific or hypothetico-deductive approach to assist metacognitive reasoning..." (p.188) (by contrast to)...the intuitive-humanist model... (whose) ...focus ...is intuition and the relationship between ...experience, the knowledge gained from it and how it enriches the ...decision-making process... (and in which) hypothesis testing is not used as a marker of accurate or inaccurate propositions ...(but) ...based on hunches[51]..." (p. 189)

---

Prospect-based decision-making process in particular, and utility-based decision-making in general, involves two stages:

- in the initial editing phase, possible outcomes of the decision are estimated, ranked and evaluated heuristically,
- in the follow-up evaluation phase, decisions are estimated in terms of whether or not their outcome could be quantified and computed, based on potential outcomes, gains and losses, and their respective probabilities, evaluation and result in choosing, more likely, the alternative having a higher utility.

A "pseudocertainty effect" occurs when people appear to be risk-averse or risk-acceptant depending on the amounts involved and on whether the gamble/choice/decision relates uniquely to becoming personally better off or worse off. We must note that it is also the case that prospect theory may violate first-order stochastic dominance, when one prospect might be preferred to another even if it yields a worse outcome with probability one, a situation that is overcome by the revised cumulative prospect theory (Tversky & Kahneman, 1981,1992).

51 i.e., probabilities, odds

Banning (2007, p. 191) also introduces a third model, originally proposed by O'Neil and collaborators (2005):

"...a multidimensional model that was developed from the synthesis of findings from research studies... based on a computerized decision support system that uses both hypothetico-deduction and pattern recognition as a basis of decision making...".

The argument is made that the benefits of each model are integrated, such that the O'Neil model of decision-making integrates "...*pre-encounter data*[52]...",.

The extent to which these approaches pertain to the process of making evidence-based decisions is explored in the next section below.

---

[52] which, by no means, represent the consensus statement of the best available evidence generated from a systematic review (*vide infra*).

*Chapter 3*

# REACHING EVIDENCE-BASED DECISIONS

## 3.1. EVIDENCE-BASED DECISION-MAKING

Based on the preceding discussion, it can be said that decisions are most often reached by means of incorporating, consciously or unconsciously, observation and evidence of some sort to a given intellectual or psycho-social schemata. Most often, decision-making is a process based on the evidence, in the sense that it incorporates this or that bit of evidence that best seems to fit our view at the time, or that we, as the decision-maker, have identified as pertinent to the case.

Decision-making based on the evidence is not evidence-based decision-making. Whereas the former is based on selected elements of the available evidence, the latter utilizes a systematic process of gathering all of the available evidence, and of screening out the problematic evidence so as to retain and to synthesize only the best available evidence. Evidence-based decision-making refers to the process of decision-making that rests on the foundation of the science of research synthesis[53] (Littell et al, 2008), and the systematic review of the evidence as its principal research tool.

The systematic review is the instrument of choice for the dissemination of the best available evidence used in making decisions in health care, in economics, in correction law, in all fields, including sustainability. Sustainable evidence-based decisions rest upon the foundations of research synthesis, systematic reviews, and the analytical tests best suited to evaluate the power and stringency of the evidence. These statistical tests are acceptable sampling and meta-analysis/-

---

[53] For completion purposes, it is recommended that this section be read while consulting the Manual (Chiappelli, 2008) (cf.,www.novapublishers.com/catalog/product_info.php?products_id=5937) in parallel.

regression, which are discussed to some depth below and elsewhere (e.g., Chiappelli, 2008; Chiappelli et al, 2009b).

The systematic review is not similar to the traditional literature, or narrative review, nor, in fact, is it a "review" paper *per se* at all. It is a piece of original research, which arises from a research question that defines and determines the problem under study (e.g., a given patient population, a given sustainability problem), the interventions under comparison (or under time sequence monitoring in a prediction approach) for a given outcome of interest[54]. The question is examined through a scientific process that utilizes published and unpublished research reports as the unit of research: the bibliome[55]. Identification of the sample is based on keywords[56], and scrutinized by inclusion and exclusion criteria. Systematic obtention of the sample ensures avoiding or minimizing publication bias, and other inherent limitations of the process. The data are interpreted from the perspective of Bayesian modeling in order to obtain statistical significance, infer clinical relevance and effectiveness and extract Markov estimates (e.g., Markov model)[57]. The outcome of this process is a consensus of the totality of the *best available* evidence for the purpose of elaborating revised common & practical guidelines[58] (rCPG's) (Chiappelli, 2008).

The process by which the available evidence is gathered in response to a given clinical or societal question, and rigorously evaluated, following the stringent protocols of research synthesis (RS) (Littell et al, 2008), for obtaining the best available evidence is sometimes referred to as evidence-based research (EBR), which in turns empowers the decision-makers to carry out evidence-based decisions (EBD).

---

54 The research question of a research synthesis/systematic review study is expressed by the acronym: P.I.C/P.O. – problem, intervention, comparison/prediction, outcome

55 the "bibliome", the totality of published research text corpus, as so defined in the biological sciences by the European Bioinformatics Institute (2000), and used often interchangeably with the somewhat less frequently used synonyms, literaturome and textome.

56 in health care research, keywords are often referred to as Medical Subject Headings (MeSH)

57 This is usually achieved by means of the Markov model-based decision tree. This approach permits to model events that may occur in the future as a direct effect of treatment or as a side effect. The model produces a decision tree that cycles over fixed intervals in time, and incorporates probabilities of occurrence. Even if the difference between the two treatment strategies appears quantitatively small, the Markov model outcome reflects the optimal clinical decision, because it is based on the best possible values for probabilities and utilities incorporated in the tree. The outcome produced by the Markov decision analysis results from the sensitivity analysis to test the stability over a range probability estimates, and thus reflects the most rational treatment choice (Yu et al, 2003; Sugar et al, 2004).

58 Common because shared among the reports examined in the bibliome under study, and practical because of direct and immediate utility and usability. In evidence-based health care (cf.,

The best available evidence that is gathered through EBR is meant to complement, not to replace the set of elements that the professional utilizes in decision-making. EBD is simply intended to formulate recommendations[59]

EBD fundamentally incorporates into decisions for specific interventions and for updating policies a plethora of well-articulated information about, such as:

- the unit of research:
  - history
  - societal wants and needs
  - results of preliminary and exploratory tests
- the decision-maker:
  - field training, expertise
  - judgment, experience
  - recommendations by colleagues, experts, governing bodies
- utility concerns:
  - risk/benefit ratio
  - cost/benefit ratio
  - insurance and payment, budget, funding (i.e., donations, grants)
- research evidence:
  - consensus of the best available research evidence following systematic reviews and meta-analyses (research synthesis process)
  - revised common & practical guidelines (rCPG's)

In addition to the Manual from this publisher (Chiappelli, 2008), a second guide to evidence-based decision-making for dental professionals has seen press, which presented a step-by-step process for making evidence-based decisions in

---

Chiappelli, 2008), rCPG's stand for revised clinical practice guidelines, which of course, are both common and practical clinical guidelines.

59 For instance in the field of dentistry, the American Dental Association (ADA) Board of Trustees examined this new approach to common & practical and sustainable solutions, and adopted resolution (B-18-1999) in February 1999 as: "...an approach to treatment planning and subsequent dental therapy that requires the judicious melding of systematic assessments of scientific evidence relating to the unit of research's medical condition and history, the dentist's clinical experience, training and judgment and the unit of research's treatment needs and preferences". The ADA further stated that "...evidence-based clinical recommendations are intended to provide guidance, and are not a standard of care, requirement or regulation...(they serve as) a resource for dentists...Rather, the EBD process is based on integrating the scientific basis for clinical care, using thorough, unbiased reviews and the best available scientific evidence at any one time, with clinical and unit of research factors to make the best possible decision(s) about appropriate health care for specific clinical circumstances. EBD relies on the role of individual professional judgment in this process..." (ADA Positions & Statements).

dental practice (Forrest et al, 2008). The model, which can evidently be extended for use in the domain of sustainability at large, consists of five distinct levels of mastery, and is an expansion of the stepwise approach developed in the Manual (Chiappelli, 2008) :

- **formulating** unit of research-centered questions – i.e., the PICO question
- **searching** for the appropriate bibliome – i.e., the initial step of research synthesis
- **critically appraising** the evidence – i.e., the core of research synthesis - the rigor of process of research integration and synthesis (i.e., inclusion & exclusion criteria; level and quality evidence[60]) (Littell et al, 2008);
- **pooling** the data from separate reports, when appropriate, for meta-analysis, meta-regression, individual unit of research data analyses, and acceptable sampling statistics (Nieri et al, 2003; Reeves et al, 2006; Chiappelli, 2008; Littell et al, 2008; CRD, 2009);
- **elaborating** of common & practical guidelines for applying the evidence consensus to practical solutions
- **evaluating** the process - i.e., evaluating outcomes and policies by normative and summative protocols

A more recent and up-to-date elaboration of the evidence-based model, its research intricacies, and its relationship to the logic conceptualization of decision-making is also to be found in Chiappelli & Cajulis (2009).


## Let Us Examine the Following Example:

Let us imagine the following societal query:

1. **PICO question**: in a problem situation (e.g., urban planning, emission control, quality of life, cost, etc.) such as a public transportation in metropolitan Los Angeles connecting the San Fernando Valley and the communities of Van Nuys, Encino, Pacoima, etc. to the Westside (Santa Monica, Westwood and UCLA and the west-Los Angeles Veterans hospital, and Los Angeles international airport) is an expansion of the

---

60 cf., criteria for the level of evidence, and the 'strength of recommendation taxonomy grading (SORT) guidelines' offered in the forward of the Journal of Evidence-Based Dental Practice, and are discussed in details in Chiappelli & Cajulis, 2009.

405 freeway recommended[61] over connecting the Orange metro line (Sepulveda or Van Nuys station) in Pacoima & the Valley to the Green line metro terminal proximal to the airport (Aviation/LAX station) by means of a line running over the existing 405[62], in terms of cost effectiveness, traffic reduction, quality of life, noise control, etc…

That PICO question is *per se* an example. But, *de facto*, and *per alterum*, a similarly posed PICO question yielded the systematic review by Lin, which studied the effect of "intelligent transport systems" on travel time in Adelaide, Australia (Lin et al, 2005).

2.  **Search Strategy:** The bibliomic search strategy needs to be all-encompassing, in order to eliminate or minimize publication bias (Moradi et al, 2006; Chiappelli, 2008), and also requires vigilant surveillance and updates (Chiappelli, 2008; Sampson et al, 2008). It needs to be refined by strict inclusion and exclusion criteria, such as, for example, narrative reviews, pre-existing systematic reviews, abstracts, unpublished reports, dissertations, and publications in press are excluded. But, reports in foreign languages are included, thus requiring critical readers[63] in foreign languages. This latter feature is essential to ensure a global perspective on the sustainability issue under consideration.

3.  **Level of evidence and quality of evidence:** Level of evidence must be determined as per standard criteria in evidence-based research (cf., note 8), but, quality of evidence must be assessed as well. The level of the evidence analysis[64], while often informative in health care systematic reviews, yields little or no relevant information in clinical situations where randomized blinded trials are all but impossible, or in the myriad of scientific domains that can & do rely on systematic reviews, but where clinical trials are not pertinent[65]. One example of a well-calibrated and

---

61 recently debated and voted by the Los Angeles City Council

62 as commonly observed in other metropolis such as San Francisco, Chicago, New York, etc.

63 multiple readers (at least two) are required, whose critical skills need to be standardized. Inter-rater reliability (Pearson correlation coefficient) and extent of agreement (Cohen kappa coefficient of agreement) serve to establish critical reading homogeneity (cf., Chiappelli, 2008).

64 We discuss elsewhere how insufficient, and in fact scientifically grossly negligent it is to assess only the level of evidence (i.e., the "what was the design of the study"), and to ignore assessing the quality of the evidence (i.e., "how well" was the design of the study conducted based on generally accepted standards of research methodology, research design and research data analysis) (Chiappelli, 2008; Chiappelli & Cajulis, 2008, 2009; Chiappelli et al, 2009b).

65 conceptually, the field has evolved in recent years in the sense of developing new tools for assessing the quality of observations studies (Stroop et al, 2000). Ongoing work in our research

validated tool for that purpose is the revised Wong (R-Wong) scale (Chiappelli, 2008). Full standardization and validation of R-Wong was described elsewhere (Chiappelli et al, 2006). At least two readers, trained and standardized in the critical assessment of the principles of research methodology, design and statistical analysis (Chiappelli, 2008), must review each report in a blind and independent protocol. Inter-rater reliability can thus be verified by Pearson r correlation coefficient and Cohen k coefficient of agreement as described in Chiappelli (2008). Divergent scores are resolved by a third reader until consensus is reached.

4.  **Data Analysis:** Acceptable sampling analysis (cf. Table 1 as an example) is performed using the Friedman test for non-parametric analysis of factorial designs, followed by Man-Whitney U post-hoc comparisons, and Bonferroni correction of the level of significance ($\alpha=0.05$) as needed. We find that the expanded excel (Analyse-It, 1997-2009; analyse-it.com) and the MDAS statistical software (Medical Data Analysis System, EsKay Software, Pittsburgh, 2004) are useful software programs for that purpose. In brief, scores from both readers are tabulated across the nine domains of research methodology, design and data analysis assessed by the R-Wong scale. Marginal totals are utilized to establish the level of acceptability within a 95% confidence interval (CI95). The relative strength of each domain is described by their respective means and coefficient of variation, and inclusion within the respective CI95 for each domain, and compared across the bibliome under study, when needed by a Wilcoxon analysis. Acceptable research findings for clinical use require high standards, and reports that are tainted by weaknesses in the domains widely recognized as fundamental criteria of sound clinical research must be excluded. Routinely, reports of excellent-good quality score 22-27 on the R-Wong; reports of weak quality obtain a 18-21 R-Wong score; and reports whose R-Wong score is below 18 are deemed unacceptable. The marginal totals (e.g., vertical marginal values, Table 1) reveal that all the studies analyzed were of acceptable quality (total score of 18 or above). A percent estimate of the reports in the bibliome can be estimated to be of excellent-good quality (score > 22), based on the total R-Wong score, and their position relative to the quality of evidence scores at CI95 determined by the population mean$\pm$ standard deviation can be estimated (e.g., bibliome average score: $21\pm2.47$; CI95: 16-26).

---

group is presently laying the foundations for stringent systematic reviews of fundamental experimental research and participant observation field research.

Systematic reviews can be assessed for quality in the same fashion using the revised form of the AMSTAR[66] (Shea et al, 2007a,b), which, as the R-Wong, generates scores for every dimension assessed as well as an overall score. The acceptable sampling analysis proceeds in the identical manner for the R-AMSTAR as for the R-Wong.

The methodological strength of the acceptable sampling analysis using an instrument such as the R-Wong or the R-AMSTAR lies in the fact that analysis of the marginal means and standard deviations (horizontal marginal values in Table 1 for R-Wong), yields invaluable information with respect to the relative strength or weakness of a given bibliome of original primary research (i.e., R-Wong) or existing systematic reviews. When the reports within a research bibliome are uniformly strong along the nine domains of the R-Wong (or the R-AMSTAR), then a Friedman analysis of the tabulated scores will not be statistically significant. A significant outcome, by contrast, indicates that some domains are strong and acceptable, but others are weak and alarming within the bibliome under study. Analysis of the strength of the evidence for the individual domains of the R-Wong (or R-AMSTAR) can indicate a significant degree of variability within the bibliome.

**Table 1. Example of acceptable sampling analysis**

| References | 1 | 2 | 3 | 4 | 5 | 6 | 7 | 8 | 9 | Total |
|---|---|---|---|---|---|---|---|---|---|---|
| a | 3.0 | 1.5 | 1.0 | 2.5 | 2.5 | 3.0 | 2.5 | 2.0 | 2.5 | 19.0 |
| b | 3.0 | 2.5 | 3.0 | 3.0 | 2.0 | 3.0 | 2.5 | 2.5 | 3.0 | 26.0 |
| c | 3.0 | 2.5 | 1.0 | 3.0 | 2.5 | 2.0 | 2.5 | 1.0 | 1.5 | 18.0 |
| d | 3.0 | 2.5 | 1.0 | 3.0 | 2.5 | 3.0 | 3.0 | 1.5 | 2.5 | 21.0 |
| e | 3.0 | 2.5 | 2.0 | 2.5 | 2.0 | 2.0 | 2.0 | 2.5 | 1.5 | 21.0 |
| f | 3.0 | 3.0 | 2.0 | 3.0 | 1.5 | 3.0 | 2.5 | 2.5 | 1.5 | 23.0 |
| mean | 3.00 | 2.42 | 1.67 | 2.83 | 2.17 | 2.67 | 2.50 | 2.00 | 2.08 | 21.33 |
| SD | 0.00 | 0.49 | 0.82 | 0.26 | 0.41 | 0.52 | 0.32 | 0.63 | 0.66 | 2.88 |

Friedman $X^2$ value:    23.7
p value                        0.0026

That is to say, typically, if the *corpus* of the literature under examination is uniformly strong or weak within a given domain tested by the R-Wong, the horizontal marginal standard deviation will be small, and the coefficient of variation will be <10% of the mean. Coefficient variations above 15% or 20% of

66 Kung et al, 2009 in  press

the mean alert to the presence of outliers: that is to say, whereas all the reports may score strongly on a given domain, one or a few particular papers will have a low score on that domain. That situation points the researcher to review carefully the grounds for inclusion and acceptability of that outlier report in the overall conclusive consensus statement of the systematic review. Post-hoc analysis of the marginal means and standard deviations (horizontal marginal values) can be used to determine which domain is significantly strong or significantly weak, and within or outside of the upper 95% confidence limit (1.80-2.88) (exceptionally strong), or lower than the lower 95% confidence limit (exceptionally weak). Further analysis can also establish whether or not a given domain is rated significantly lower in one subset of the bibliome, compared to the other by using a Wilcoxon nonparametric comparison. Quality of the evidence assessments, when performed by a well-constructed and standardized instrument that captures the widely accepted domains of the scientific process, can generate important observations with respect to general acceptability of reports.

Acceptable and homogeneous reports can then be incorporated in a meta-analysis of the outcome. That is to say, based upon the outcome of the acceptable sampling, a fixed-model meta-analysis may be conducted. Several useful softwares exist for that purpose, among which we have found Comprehensive Meta-analysis by Biostat Inc., (meta-analysis.com, 2006) to be practical. Meta-analysis is the preferred protocol for over-arching analysis of statistical trends in evidence-based research, because it seeks to combine all the relevant results found from the literature identified to produce more precise results than the individual studies.

Insuring inclusion only of homogeneous and acceptable reports from a systematic review in the meta-analysis yields adequate statistical stringency and power to unveil a significant effect, if there is one to be seen. Nevertheless, important caveats remain, particularly with respect to its use in preliminary systematic review where the size of the bibliome *corpus* under examination is low. Issues of heterogeneity, as determined by the Cochran Q and the $I^2$ analyses, cannot be avoided in case of a small sample size. Issues of publication bias also cannot be verified by L'Abbé or funnel plots when the sample size of meta-analysis is small, and can be prohibitively pervasive in such preliminary systematic reviews. The multiplicity of independent and control variables may further confound data interpretation, and it is important to develop and to validate standards for the evaluation of the quality and reliability of systematic reviews and meta-analysis[67].

---

67 e.g., quality of reporting of meta-analysis, QUOROM and PRISMA

Sensitivity analysis ought to follow a well-conducted meta-analysis in order to assess the robustness of the research synthesis review results by repeating the analysis with adjustments, such as exclusion of studies with unclear or inadequate allocation concealment, and absent, unclear or inadequate blinding.

As the bibliome grows, multiple systematic reviews are produced in response to any given PICO question, which brings into sharper focus the need, urgency and utility in the context of fast emerging reliance of our societal system on sustainable CER[68] and EBD[69]. In some instances, multiple systematic reviews are concordant in the generated consensus statements; in other instances, discordant systematic reviews may arise. In either instance, it is becoming increasingly important to refine research synthesis tools to evaluate the overall evidence across multiple systematic reviews toward the generation of "complex systematic" reviews (Whitlock et al, 2008) or "meta-systematic reviews" (Chiappelli et al, 2009). It must also be noted that, as more systematic reviews are published on a given topic, the Bayesian meta-analytical inference model will most likely be the model of choice since, any new systematic review evidence contributes to yielding a ("posterior") distribution for the newly elaborated "complex" meta-analysis, which itself becomes the new "prior" distribution awaiting addition of the next meta-analysis to the model – provided, of course, that all the necessary assumptions have been satisfied. Formative and summative evaluation (Hastings and Madaus, 1971) must be obtained at key capstone time-points in order to ensure steady progress toward obtaining anticipated outputs, and desired outcomes, and, in the final analysis, toward providing justification for testing the model experimentally in any given situation in the first place.

In summary, sustainable EBD and CER rest on the consensus of the best available evidence to revise common & practical guidelines, protocols, and policies. Because the instruments and the process utilized to reach that consensus must be scrutinized, evaluated and standardized, it is imperative that systematic reviews be of high quality and follow a rigorous, the detailed and tested research synthesis protocol, including for the acceptable sampling and meta-analytical processing of the data (Chiappelli, 2008; Littell et al, 2008). It follows that evidence-based practice (EBPr) for the implementation of sustainable decisions calls for standards and instruments of evaluation. One such approach is provided by GRADE[70] (Guyatt et al, 2008), a validated approach for going from research

---

68 e.g., Threshold and Prioritization Criteria Outlined by the Federal Coordinating Council for Comparative Effectiveness Research
69 these two fields, while distinct, represent two sides of the same coin (Chiappelli et al, 2009b).
70 'appraisal of guidelines, research and evaluation – Europe' (AGREE) instrument (Cluzeau et al, 2003; Faggion, 2008).

evidence to clinical intervention, and for assessing the quality of evidence for diagnostic recommendations (GRADE, 2004; Guyatt et al, 2008; Schünemann et al, 2008). GRADE addresses issues of concern to units of research , clinicians, and, to some extent, policy makers. GRADE provides a sound evaluative assessment of evidence-based interventions for outcomes such as the quality of evidence for each outcome, the relative importance of outcomes, the overall quality of evidence, the balance of benefits, harms and costs, and considers the strength of recommendation and the overall value of implementation[71].

## 3.2. EVIDENCE-BASED VS. COMPARATIVE EFFECTIVENESS RESEARCH

Comparative effectiveness research (CER[72]) is a type of health care research that contrasts the results of one approach for managing a disease to the results of other approaches, and often compares two or more types of clinical diagnoses, procedures or protocols, in an effort to standardize quality, improve outcomes, and control costs. A new Federal Coordinating Council for Comparative Effectiveness Research has been established, and considerable funding has been released by the US for the performance of CER. The WHO also promotes and supports CER efforts in developed and in developing countries (Bates et al, 2009). This research promises to fill important information gaps facing clinicians, units of research, and third-party providers concerning what is the best and most cost effective treatment.

There remains, however, some concerns that CER cannot, by its own nature, take adequate account of individual unit of research differences, and that it consequently might impede the development and establishment of personalized health care (Garber & Tunis, 2009). This point of skepticism might be warranted, particularly when CER is taken as an end to itself.

A more complete conceptualization of health care in the XXI Century, however, considers that CER is intimately intertwined with, and cannot be torn apart from evidence-based practice (EBPr) in health care. As EBPr strives to

---

71 As discussed in Chiappelli & Cajulis, 2009, an obligatory step that follows evidence-based decision-making is implementation of policies (e.g., sustainable policies). Our group is developing an expanded GRADE that will proffer evaluation assessment of evidence-based policies.
72 HHS Secretary Kathleen Sebelius (HHS Press Office, Monday, June 29, 2009) has also refered to CER as "unit of research centered research" (www.hhs.gov/news/press/2009pres/06/20090629a.html)

apply evidence-based decisions toward the resolution of the problem situation identified in the PIC/PO question, CER seeks to determine which specific groups or types of resolutive interventions in terms of cost might benefit, with an emphasis on financial implications.

EBPr and CER are two sides of the same coin: one pertains to efficacy of personalized interventions (e.g., health care), and the other addresses cost burden and effectiveness. Cost–benefit analysis is the primary finality of CER; but EBPr is primarily concerned with resolution of the PIC/PO query from an intervention perspective, and overall outcomes satisfaction (e.g., QoL, SoL). CER and EBPr work in tandem, in a complementary and synergistic fashion for society's best interests.

The decision-making process in EBPr follows essentially the logic model, whereas decisions are most often derived in CER by means of the utilitarian model (Chiappelli & Cajulis, 2009). However, both EBPr and CER, being two distinct facets of one and the same pragmatic drive to advance our knowledge about the efficacy and cost-effectiveness of strategies, rest on the integration of recommendations obtained and derived from the best available research evidence. This integration step is accomplished by a decision support systems that work seamlessly with practice aids, and personal electronic records.

CER has been designed as a type of research that compares the results of one approach for managing a problem to the results of other approaches. Presently, CER sees its major applications in the filed of health care – perhaps in part because of the heated ongoing debate on health care reform -, consequently the overwhelming focus of what is being discussed today pertains to CER in health care. That is not to say that CER does not apply to other fields: in fact it does, and to a very important extent.

Case in point, this type of research has been conducted, supported and sponsored by the Agency for Healthcare Research and Quality (AHRQ) within the US Public Health Service to focus specifically on effectiveness research. This agency was formed by the Omnibus Budget Reconciliation Act of 1989 (Public Law 101-239) and was originally called the Agency for Health Care Policy and Research.

CER usually compares two or more types of interventions for a given societal concern by means of a process we ought to be quite familiar with at this juncture:

- PI/PO as the hypothesis-driven query
- Search and identification of the pertinent bibliome
- Critical analysis of the level and quality of the evidence

- Data analysis by means of acceptable sampling and meta-analysis/-regression
- Inferences in the form of consensus-recommended common and practical guidelines

Followed by:

- Evaluation of outcomes (i.e., GRADE)
- Elaboration of policies
- Evaluation of the evidence-based policies (Ex-GRADE)

More generally, clearinghouses for comparative effectiveness and best available evidence data are established across numerous professional fields, as we noted, from environmental studies, to economics, and act in concert to help government officials, policymakers, researchers, and professionals make better informed decisions. Because cost–benefit analysis is a primary end of CER and evidence-based decision (EBD) is primarily concerned with effectiveness and satisfaction (i.e., QoL, SoL), they have the potential to work synergistically for the unit of research's and society's best interests in a new world driven not by use, abuse and waste, but by re-cycle, re-use and sustain.

Once the CER studies have been completed and analyzed, the results must be evaluated for their usefulness to improve clinical decision-making. Getting the information to the unit of stakeholders when and where they need it, when they need it and in a format that is efficient and user friendly must be part of the effort to improve societal solutions in health care. This critical integration step is accomplished by clinical decision support (CDS) systems that have the ability to work seamlessly with practice aids, electronic records and devices. Integrating CDS into the workflow will make the information derived from CER both useful and important.

## 3.3. SUMMARY: EVIDENCE-BASED DECISION-MAKING

We argued above that the final stage of EBD concerns evidence-based policies (EBPo), which still requires the validation of an evaluative instruments that may extend and expand GRADE to include assessment of policies, because the evidence-based practice environment is that it must support and promote the use of best evidence by requiring common & practical policies and procedures to be evidence-based (Oman et a, 2008). The expanded version of GRADE (Ex-GRADE), which we, at present, are endeavoring in validating (Chiappelli et al, 2009c), includes the fundamental elements of policy evaluation that have been current in health care practice for the last decade (Gilbert and Taylor, 1999), and that can be outlined as:

- What is the extent of relevance to practice?
- Are the condition and interventions specific?
- Is the target population well defined?
- How good is the policy's evidence?
- What biases does the policy reflect
- Is the policy ready to implement?

- by assembling a team and building consensus
- by documenting all intervention processes
- by modifying the policy for local use
- by communicating changes in processes
- by establishing modalities to evaluate the policy
- by testing possible changes or interventions
- by adopting the revised clinical policy
- by evaluating the new policy

In brief, the strength of the logic model for its application to evidence-based decision-making rests in its inherent property to formulate in quantifiable terms the emerging situation, the required action-response, and the concrete results. As noted above, the model provides invaluable normative and summative evaluation of the evidence as part of a framework for describing the relationships between investments/inputs, activities and results. It yields a concrete approach for integrating planning, implementation, evaluation and reporting.

Evidence-based decision-making is based upon the application of the scientific method of research synthesis for the conscientious, explicit and judicious use of current best evidence, evaluated by a systematic process of the level *and* the quality of the research evidence. Systematic reviews provide a tool to apply stringent scientific strategies to quantify the quality of the accumulated research evidence, and limit bias. They utilize and integrate both acceptable analysis and meta-analysis to establish the level of overall significance of the gathered evidence, and are vastly different in purpose and format from narrative reviews and health technology assessments (Chiappelli & Cajulis, 2008).

In its simplest elaboration, as in its most complex iteration, the logic model of decision-making has fundamental strengths that set it apart for other models. From the perspective of the initial consideration of the task, it permits to forge a master plan that "sees" the end, that does more than simply consider inputs or tasks, but that visualizes and focuses upon the ultimate outcomes and the results to be gained. The logic model is a proactive approach to identify the optimal procedural steps to achieve the desired results, and to prove the working hypothesis under study. It permits focus on accountability for investment based on long-term outcomes (Engle-Cox et al, 2009).

Furthermore, the logic model, which needs not be linear, provides sound indicators of finality, in terms of output and outcome measures of performance (i.e., work-hours, manpower), as well as success. Short-term, intermediate as well as long-term outcomes are clearly identifiable. This permits to set criteria for immediate and for mission success far in the future. In these cases, intermediate or shorter-term outcomes may be identified that provide an indication of progress toward the ultimate long-term outcome. Therefore, and most importantly, as elaborated above, the logic model has, intertwined within each of its steps, reliable formative and summative evaluative protocols that can be integrated at every step.

In Part II, we discussed several of the tenets of the process of evidence-based decision-making[73] as it rests on seven fundamental contingencies

- recognition of the research's problem
- construction of a structured PIC/PO question
- thorough search of pertinent literature and bibliome

---

73 This has sometimes been referred to as "intelligent" evidence-based decision-making, which distinguishes "collectors", "processors", and "analysts", and proceeds as follows:

directive phase:the specific 'intelligence question' is posed – in the preceding chapter, we indicated that the directive phase of the evidence-based process is the statement of the PICO question.

collection phase:the data, information, processed intelligence and corporate 'wisdom' resides – in the context of evidence-based decision-making, we stressed the need to integrate expertise and experience with the entire body of available evidence.

analysis phase:the collected information is collated, analyzed and evaluated. This is identical to the step we described in the previous chapter where the best evidence is obtained from the entire body of available evidence, based on the level and the quality of the evidence, followed by acceptable sampling and meta-analysis.

dissemination phase: the processed information, data and intelligence is presented in a form that is useful, relevant, in context and most importantly timely. This step corresponds, for all intents and purposes, to the systematic review format of reporting the evidence-based process.

reflection phase:the newly discovered information is incorporated into corporate wisdom and from which flows new and improved questions and tasks. The evidence-based paradigm here speaks of the dissemination of the consensus of revised guidelines.

- evaluation of the evidence for quality and level of evidence
- retrieval of the best available evidence to answer the question
- critical appraisal of all available evidence into revised clinical guidelines
- integration with all aspects and contexts of sustainable decision-making

The consensus of the total best available evidence is obtained and utilized cogently in making evidence-based decisions that pertain to the specific intervention called for in the PIC/PO question. But, one fundamental question remains: how do we "translate" the evidence derived from group data, as commonly obtained in research studies and synthesized in systematic reviews and meta-analyses, to have any degree of pertinence and direct applicability to sustainable solutions.

We described the process of engagement of the systematic reviews as a tool to apply stringent scientific strategies to quantify the quality of the accumulated research evidence in order to limit bias during the application of this evidence to the resolution of societal problems. Systematic reviews utilize and integrate both acceptable analysis and meta-analysis to establish the level of overall significance of the gathered evidence, and are therefore vastly different from narrative reviews and health technology assessments.

It follows that common & practical guidelines in general, and specifically in the realm of sustainable solutions are systematically developed statements that aim to provide decision-makers and health care providers (i.e., in the present context, sustainable solutions providers), and insurance coverage providers with the best available updated information to optimize decisions. The guidelines must incorporate validity, reliability, reproducibility, practical applicability and flexibility, clarity, development through a multidisciplinary process, scheduled reviews, and documentation. Evidence-based common and practical guidelines must therefore represent statements developed to improve the quality of sustainable solutions, unit of research access, treatment outcomes, appropriateness of care, efficiency and effectiveness and achieve cost containment by improving the cost benefit ratio.

Evidence is knowledge. And knowledge is a commodity that has three basic components, which are used to obtain sustainable evidence-based decisions in the political, the economic, the social, the health care, or any other societal realm with agenda-based purposes, such as equity, spending accountability, and reduction in variability. Arbitrating the decision process in an evidence-based paradigm is to consider all relevant influences that may impact on the management and use of knowledge in making evidence-based decisions (EBD).

In the context of sustainable solutions, the best available evidence thus becomes a service tool used to measure the number of people served and the cost of the services, which in turn can provide support for political decisions to include or exclude certain dental benefits, solutions and interventions. Allocation of public monies for these benefits must be accountable to the public, and the best available evidence can be used (*nota bene,* and abused) to justify, justly or unjustly, spending based on actual or politically perceived rights. Evidence-based decision-making is a useful, albeit potentially dangerous, societal and political tool to manipulate socio-economic policies aimed at diverting funding and support for necessary coverage for sustainable solutions. These interventions aim to benefit certain groups of citizens, but may also serve to the detriment of others[74] (Bauer et al, 2006).

In the public sector dominated by insurance and investments instruments, EBD and CER are largely sensitive to costs and numbers. In the private sector, ruled primarily by the wealth of the individual unit of research, evidence-based decision-making is driven understandably so more by commodity and unit of research wants, than by the societal economics coverage (Donaldson et al, 2002; Chiappelli & Cajulis, 2009). In both instances, shared evidence-based decision-making tends to increase unit of research motivation and compliance, and to decrease the possibility of litigation (Bauer et al, 2006). In an effort to define sustainable evidence-based decisions, in general, solutions are obtained by either an intuitive or an analytical approach (Bauer et al, 2006; Chiappelli et al, 2009a).

- the *intuitive approach* applies to those situations in which the presenting condition and unit of research characteristics are consistent with findings that are associated with predictable outcomes, mental model of categories of action, and an overall concept of intervention modalities (cf., logic and rationality).
- the *analytic approach* applies specifically to those presenting conditions and query characteristics that are less certain, and require inferences about modalities benefits, costs and harms are variable, unknown (cf., uncertainty and risk).

As stated at the onset of this discussion, some among the most reliable processes of decision-making are grounded on tenets of cognitive psychology,

---

74 well then, the argument that the evidence-based process is a "conspiracy" of some sort may not be completely untenable, when viewed under this light.

reason, rationality and logic[75]. We noted that the framework referred to as the Logic Model permits focus on accountability for investment based on long-term outcomes (Engle-Cox et al, 2009), and, by consisting of the logic model, it analyzes work into four distinct intertwined and logically flowing categories[76], which mirror the evidence-based process (Mayeske & Lambur, 2001). How then this pertains to making sustainable decisions merits further reflection.

---

75 By definition, logic is the science and the study of the principles of valid demonstration and inference developed by the ancient (India, China, Arabia), and eventually articulated by Aristotle, and which became the foundation of the modern Western scientific endeavor, probability theory and statistical inference, computer science and artificial intelligence. To be grounded in logic, an argument must rest on elements that are consistent, sound and complete. The argument may follow from given premises, and be deductive in nature; or it may reliably derive generalization from observations, and be inductive. Informal logic, such as that espoused by Plato, is the study of natural language arguments. The process of deriving a Aristotelian formal logic concerns inferences with purely formal, albeit explicit content (cf., Oragnon & Prior Analytics). Symbolic predicate and propositional logic pertains to symbolic abstractions that capture the formal features of logical inference. Mathematical logic extends the boundaries of symbolic logic beyond the confines of language. Sir Michael AE Dummett (1925 - ), leading British thinker, Hilary W Outnam (1926), Donald Davidson (1917-2003) and Saul Kripke (1940), leading American thinkers, and Alfred Traski (1901-1983), leading Polish thinker, are regarded as the foremost contemporary philosophers of logic.

76 The US academic system (i.e., University Cooperative Extension Programs) has developed a five-step more complex variation of the logic model (i.e., the Program Action Logic Model): a) situations (i.e., budgetary, academic priorities), b) inputs (i.e., what we invest, what we need), c) activities (i.e., what needs to be done, what is de facto done), d) outputs (i.e., measurable outcomes), e) outcomes (i.e., budgetary and academic impact) – these can be measured on the short term (e.g., learning, skills, motivation, GPA), on the medium term (e.g., behavioral changes, policies), and on the long term (e.g., social, economic, and environmental consequences).

*Chapter 4*

# TOWARD SUSTAINABLE
# EVIDENCE-BASED DECISIONS

## 4.1. SUSTAINABLE DECISIONS

In the clinical sciences, homeostasis is defined as the property of biological systems to regulate their biochemical, cellular and physiological internal environments in order to maintain a stable, constant *milieu interieur*. This dogma was proposed by the French physiologist, Claude Bernard[77] in 1865.

Over the past 150 years, research has shown and confirmed that homeostasis is constantly and consistently threatened by environmental demands (e.g., adaptation to toxic substances, cold, hunger, etc.), as well as by forces from within the individual, such as invading pathogens, psycho-emotional stress, and the like. The organism strives to remain stable by large and fine variations, modulations and changes in certain physiological processes, in a concerted action toward regaining constancy of the *milieu interieur*. In biological systems, the process of remaining stable (ſ ſ || ſſ, histēmi, Gk, *standing still*) by being variable (allo, allo, Gk, *different*) is referred to as allostasis[78]. Homeostasis and allostasis work in

---

77 Claude Bernard (12 July 1813 – 10 February 1878) authored La fixité du milieu intérieur est la condition d'une vie libre et indépendante (The constancy of the internal environment is the condition for a free and independent life), published in Paris, 1865.
78 The concept of allostasis, maintaining stability through change, is a fundamental process through which organisms actively adjust to both predictable and unpredictable events. Sterling P, Eyer J. Allostasis: A new paradigm to explain arousal pathology. In: S. Fisher and J. Reason (Eds.), Handbook of Life Stress, Cognition and Health. 1988, John Wiley & Sons, New York. Chiappelli F, Prolo P, Fiala M, Cajulis O, Iribarren J, Panerai A, Neagos N, Younai F, Bernard G. Allostasis in HIV Infection and AIDS. In Neuro-AIDS. PA Minagar & P Shapshak, Eds. Nova Science Publisher, Inc. 2006 Chapter VI pp. 121-65.

tandem as complementary endogenous systems responsible for maintaining the internal stability of a biological organism[79]. To a similar extent, in a sustainable society, people are rarely subject to conditions that systematically undermine their capacity to meet their own needs. Rather, individuals are part of a much larger complex system, and work in a concerted effort toward proactive solutions that address the source of the original societal and ecological problem, as opposed to the effects of it on single entities.

A "sustainable biosphere[80]" is one driven by the inter-connection and the inter-dependence between its participating individuals, within its cultural, ecological and environmental context to integrate social, economic, and environmental considerations in a strategic and holistic way. Ideally, individuals within a sustainable biosphere take decisions that are directed both inward toward the betterment of their quality of life (QoL) and standard of living (SoL) within the biosphere, as well as outwardly for improving interplay, cross-feeding and enrichment across the "universe" of inter-related biospheres.

This modern and contemporary view of sustainability and sustainable decisions arose in large part from the seminal work by the Club of Rome[81] in 1972, the Brundtland commission[82] in 1987, and the Natural Step[83] in 1989. The

---

79 The psycho-social sciences have a similar paradigm to explain and to measure the fit of the person (i.e., inner & outer worlds, perceived vs. real) with the environment (i.e., perceived vs. real). The tensions leading to a poor fit of the person in the environment could arise from altered reality contact, as well as from changes in the environment that are too gargantuan to comprehend, let alone to process and to become accommodated to (e.g., the "stress" of immigration, with the associated tear in the fabric of one's inner, outer and social worlds). Poor person-environment fit is often defined as "stress", and the resolution of this stress is brought about by concerted interventions aimed to the person as well as to the environment (French et al, 1974). We have used this theoretical paradigm in our studies of patients with Alzheimer's disease and their caregivers (Chiappelli et al, 2006b), in an effort to demonstrate the wide applicability of the model. The relevance and implication of the person-environment fit in the context of sustainability issues and of making sustainable decisions are evident, and now call for articulated validation research.

80 "The economy is a wholly owned subsidiary of the biosphere. The biosphere provides everything that makes life possible, assimilates our waste or converts it back into something we can use" (Anthony Cortese, founder and president of the sustainability education organization Second Nature).

81 The Club of Rome (clubofrome.org) is an association of the world's brightest and most influential people, who gather to discuss solutions for international issues of sustainability: a global think tank that deals with a variety of international political issues. It is renowned for its founder, Aurelio Peccei (4 July 1908 – 14 March 1984), and for its many groundbreaking programs, conferences and publications, including The Limits to Growth, 1972, and The First Global Revolution, 1993.

82 the modern sense of the word "sustainability" was coined in 1987 with the publication of Our Common Future, by the United Nations World Commission on Environment and Development, the Brundtland commission, named after its chair, Norwegian diplomat Gro Harlem Brundtland.

last two decades have witnessed major elaborations and clarifications upon these early positions on sustainability for the pursuance of progress and the betterment of society.

In its last meeting in April 2009, the Club of Rome, for example, discussed the underlying causes of *un*sustainability in the world from the perspectives of the current financial, economic, environmental and development instability. It proposed lines of action to work together to develop coherent strategies to master the connected issues of climate, energy, ecosystems and water, to outline financial system reform, economic restructuring and globalization, and to control poverty by fostering international development. Thus, as discussed below (cf., 4.2), the current view of sustainability emerged as necessitating, *de facto*, the three distinct, yet intertwined interdisciplinary domains of economics, environmental sciences, and equity[84] has emerged as the preferred paradigm[85].

The current and ongoing work of The Natural Step and of the Club of Rome[86] exemplify a concerted movement of society away from the wanton abuses of the past, and toward a new horizon of collaborative effort and endeavor aimed at preserving the diversity and the integrity of societal biospheres, and, to the extent of the possible, to assist in regaining them the vigor of the past. It is a cognitive shift, a changing of views, an embracing of an awareness of the need to preserve rather than wantonly waste, it is a seeing beyond present limitations or thought patterns: it is a cognitive *metanoia*[87].

---

The report defined sustainable development as "...development that meets the needs of the present without compromising the ability of future generations to meet their own needs..."

83 The Swedish oncologist, Karl-Henrik Robèrt, led a group of 50 scientists to define the modern concept of sustainability in the early 1980's. As a product of their work and his leadership, the nonprofit organization, The Natural Step (www.naturalstep.org), was founded in Sweden in 1989, with the intent of pioneering the Backcasting from Principles approach, designed to effectively advance society towards a consensus- and systematic principle-based definition of sustainability.

84 In the sense of social, ethnic, racial, cultural, age gender, religious parity

85 societal problems require sustainable decisions to yield sustainable solutions, which must be based upon and embrace principles of economics, environmental sciences and equity.

86 For example, in its June 2008 Press Release, the Club outlined its endeavors to come as follows "...The Club will focus its activities on such issues as: the ecosystems crisis and degradation of the environment, the urgent need to move towards a low carbon economy to avert runaway climate change, the challenges of globalization and the vulnerability of the international economic and financial system, the explosive rise of prices of food and energy and the intensifying competition of a growing world population for land, water and other vital resources, rising inequality and polarization in a world of intense poverty...."

87 Grk. Metanoein: μετάνοια, that is, μετά, after, with + νοέω, to perceive, to think, and the outcome of these actions: thus, metanoia literally a change of mind

The concern for and action toward sustainable solutions[88] has never been, from an historical point of view, more timely and critical as it is at present. We live in an age of dwindling resources and raw materials for our unending and never quenched thirst and hunger for energy. And, contemporaneously, this our moment in the history of humankind and civilization is one of extensive use and abuse of energy, of production and over-production of wastes and discards of all nature and types that are toxic to the seas, the earth, the air and atmosphere, the environment at large, and our very psychobiologic health and well-being. Taken together, what some may call "the progress" of the last two hundred years, others decry as the wanton engagement of humanity in a spiral leading to the perdition of the human race, the destruction of our planet, and the elimination of life as we know it[89].

Whereas the promise of globalization was far more equitable trade, and far more evenly spread societal gains, a reality of imbalances and unfair solutions, preferential enrichments, and discriminatory impoverishments has emerged across continents, nations, trades and industries, businesses of small, medium and larges sizes, and, overall, drop in individuals' quality of life across ethnic groups, cultures and socio-economic levels. All in all, except for the few who have grown richer in the last decades, most have suffered as a direct outcome of unsustainable decisions, including the ill-conceived, ill-fated and ill-actualized process of globalization.

The pursuance of progress, modern commodities and, all in all, a comfortable life, which has characterized the activities of Western society – the so-called 1st world – since the onset of the Industrial Revolution over a 150 years ago, has led emerging societies – the "2nd world" – to seek the same for their citizens. Developing countries of less "privileged" continents – privileged, that is, from the viewpoint of the West – have a uniform view of quality of life across cultures and

---

88 This is akin and related to the horizontal phase, presencing, of the U theorized by Scharmer (2009). In his cogent conceptualization of Theory U, Professor Scharmer (MIT) discussed the descending limb of the U as a progressively increased awareness of the problem and problematic situation by means of overcoming judgment and pre-judgment, cynicism, and fear. The bottom horizontal segment of the U signifies the bridge between the present conditions that the past has brought upon the present situation, and future actions and development toward resolution. The inherent energy of the process drives to the ascending limb of the U, which permits the elaborations of novel and improved approaches. The crystallization of this vision into doable tasks and operations, and the normative and summative evaluation of prototypic strategies toward the threshold of solving the problem.

89 "...the social structures that we see decaying and crumbling – locally, regionally and globally – are built on two different sources: premodern traditional, and modern industrial structures or forms of thinking and operating. Both of them have been successful in the past. But in our current age, each disintegrates and crumbles..." (Scharmer, 2009, p.3)

societies, and seek by and large of adopting the West's as the Gold Standard of life satisfaction. That has engendered jealousy, violence, hate, war – both civil and across nations -, and terrorism. The globalization process of our way of life has led to an unsustainable spiral of progressive destruction of humanity, the variety of its cultures, the richness of its people's civilizations, and the civility of its inhabitants. Whether it was intended or not, large food chains and fast food restaurants, for example, have penetrated the fabric of societies far from where they were originally designed, and where this approach to feed self, family and population was not part of the culture. In so doing, businesses small and large, and local food detail operations were wantonly replaced, bankrupt and effaced. Societal habits that were generations-old were obliterated in a few years, and altered into interactions that were never felicitous, and more often than not brought to family dissonance and to disjointed societies. A sense of lack of productivity, deprived self-pride and diminished self-concept became pervasive as individuals emigrated away from their original cultural and ethnic cradle: families were torn and eventually destroyed, lives broken, and societies fractured. The unsustainable process of socio-ethnic erosion could not but lead to the inexorable consummation of the fundamentals of societal interactions.

As we pause now and reflect upon entering the second decade of this millennium, we must come to realize that our world is perilously engaged in an unsustainable pattern of life – a self-destructive *modus vivendi* of Take – Make – Waste. From our abuse of resources and energy, to our excess in the generation of toxic waste, to the concerted destructive effects of our societal priorities upon the ethno-cultural patrimony of humanity, our current *modus vivendi* is unsustainable and must be changed, corrected, re-directed. From our values and priorities that seek to replace spirituality with a finance- and business-based view of the world, to our relentless drive toward uniform "sameness" of mores and habits, and away from social, ethnic and cultural identity and "uniqueness", to our biased, discriminatory and prejudgmental tunnel-vision, our current *modus vivendi* is untenable and unsustainable. From our choice of violence over reason and dialogue, to our celebration of the victor at all cost over the participants for the honor to take part, to our exultation of competition rather than cooperation, our contemporary *modus vivendi* is uncivilized, untenable and unsustainable: it will, in the end – an end that is not so far in the future – destroy us and our civilizations, obliterate humanity and our environment. In brief, we must strive to solutions that transform our very thinking and acting to learn from the future as it emerges with an open mind, an open heart, and an open will[90] (Sharmer, 2009).

As harsh as this view of our current reality may appear, truth be told: many across many countries, cultures and continents in the 1st, 2nd and 3rd Worlds have forcefully and more effectively than I ever could decried this state of affairs. Many political, religious and non-denominational groups and organizations have mobilized members and sympathizers – sometimes peacefully, other times forcefully and violently – to express the need for change. Authors and poets, musicians and singers, painters and sculptors, architects, dancers, and artists of all sorts have utilized their exquisite skills across ethnic boundaries to remind us of the infinite beauty of individuality, the infinite richness of creative imagination, and of the infinite value of each one of us imbedded as we are in the infinite depth of the cultural and anthropological reality of the moment present[91].

It is undeniable that a movement toward increased realization of the urgent need for sustainable decisions is rising globally, forcefully, inexorably. Hope is in the air – "a change we can believe in" -. And mine is not an empty statement of gloom, but a call toward an articulated process of evidence-based decision-making for sustainable solutions in today's world for tomorrow

## 4.2. SUSTAINABILITY INTO THE 2ND DECADE OF THE XXI CENTURY

But, what then, one may ask, is "sustainability", and what role can it play, and will it play in the next decade?

As defined by the World Conservation Union, United Nation Environment Program (World-wide Fund for Nature, 1991), sustainability is said to comprise a complex set activities led by experts in their respective fields, and striving to

---

90 Scharmer (2009) reminds us that Aristotle presented in Book VI of Nicomachean Ethics (Τα Ετηικα), a book dedicated to Aristotle 's son, Nicomachus, the penta-nature of intellectual "virtues", our abilities to capture knowledge, and to act upon it (hence, make decisions upon it): scientific knowledge (i.e., episteme), art/productivity/creativity (i.e., techne), prudence/practicality (i.e., phronesis), intuition/capability to grasp principles (i.e., nous), and wisdom (i.e., sophia).

91 We cannot but agree with Scharmer's statement (2009, p. 22) "...all leaders and innovators, whether in business, communities, government, or nonprofit organizations, do what artists do: they create something new and bring it into the world...". This is what we are now called to do: to transform of mindset in order to make decisions that are sustainable in all aspects of life and society, and for dimensions of society. Regardless of what the past has brought us to, we must *blick nach vorn"* (look forward; Scharmer, 2009, p. 25).

*"improve the quality of human life, while living within the carrying capacity of supporting eco-systems".*

While precise, that definition may be overly concise. The sustainability movement, in the view of the original Brundtland commission report just over two decades ago, is meant to focus on finding ways to let poor nations catch up to richer ones in terms of quality of life (QoL) standard of living (SoL). That goal meant giving disadvantaged countries better access to natural resources, including water, energy and food: the "biosphere". Today, a more comprehensive view of sustainability pertains to the intersecting of three professional fields for the betterment of the survival of individuals within the biosphere: environmental science, economics, and equity (*vide supra*).

Sustainability refers to the process directed at maintaining balance within human systems: that is to say, a societal situation in which co-inhabiting members of a group do not systematically undermine the natural eco-structure of the social biosphere. It may be compared to the physiological process of maintaining homeostatic balance in a biological organism.

The strong trends in climate change already evident, the likelihood of further changes occurring, and the increasing scale of potential climate impacts give urgency to addressing adaptation more coherently. There are many potential adaptation options available for marginal change of existing global systems, often variations of existing climate risk management. Implementation of these options is likely to have substantial benefits under moderate climate change for some specific systems (e.g., agriculture, air and water quality, noise pollution). There are limits to their effectiveness under more severe climate changes.

More systemic changes in resource allocation need to be considered, such as targeted diversification of production systems and livelihoods. Achieving increased adaptation action necessitates integration of climate change-related issues with other risk factors, such as climate variability and market risk, and with other policy domains, such as sustainable development, and must be articulated with budgetary realities, priorities and projections . Dealing with the many barriers to effective adaptation requires a comprehensive and dynamic policy approach covering a range of scales and issues, for example, from the understanding by farmers of change in risk profiles to the establishment of efficient markets that facilitate response strategies. Science and economics have to adapt in tandem to bring forward societal change: they have to lead the way for the planet to lead "...*from the future as it emerges*[92]..."

---

92 Scharmer, 2009

Multidisciplinary problems require multidisciplinary solutions. In the case of sustainability, we need a focus on integrated sciences and a strengthening of the interface with decision makers. A crucial component of this approach is the implementation of adaptation assessment frameworks that are relevant, robust, and easily operated by all stakeholders, practitioners, policymakers, and scientists. One important example of action in sustainability that has timely global impact relates to the process of adapting global issues to climate change, as noted above, in an effort to preserve our environment at different latitudes, while also providing for the well-being of local and distant communities (Howden et al, 2007).

If people continue to pour carbon dioxide into the air, for example, we won't necessarily exhaust those specific resources, but we will change the climate in ways that could very likely impose huge burdens on future generations. The same, of course, goes for other poisonous by-products from all kinds of human activity, from manufacturing to mining to energy generation to agriculture, marine biology , and so on, that get dumped onto the land and into streams, oceans and the atmosphere.

In the contemporary view, sustainability goes beyond the preservation of the biosphere *per se* in that it pertains more generally to the task of preserving the quality of life (QoL) and the standard of living (SoL) for this generation, and for our children's and future generations. With some six billion people estimated on the planet by the end of the present decade, and another three billion expected by the middle of the century, societies and nations across the globe cannot sustain a satisfactory quality of life (QoL) and standard of living (SoL) for their citizens without an increasingly heavy dependence on waste-generating supplies, fuel and technologies.

Electric cars, wind turbines and solar cells utilize natural renewable resources and allow people to achieve a certain QoL and SoL while emitting fewer noxious chemicals than petroleum, natural gas, or coal. Nuclear power, unlike the other alternative energy sources, has long been problematic to environmentalists, sustainability scientists and policy makers as an alternative energy source because, in part at least, of associated problems of storing radioactive waste, and of potential for catastrophic meltdowns[93]. Nor is sustainability solely and all about

---

93 Cf., for example, on 26 April 1986, a reactor at the Chernobyl plant, near Pripyat in the Ukrainian Soviet Socialist Republic, exploded. Further explosions and the resulting fire sent a plume of highly radioactive fallout into the atmosphere and over an extensive geographical area. The fallout that was released was sizably more considerable than what had been released by the atomic bombing of Hiroshima, as it drifted over the USSR, Eastern and Western Europe, Scandinavian countries, as far west as the eastern North American shores. What was termed "nuclear rain" fell as far as Ireland. Over 600,000 people were exposed to alarmingly elevated

energy system research and development[94] replace, in most instances, costly unsustainable systems[95] already in place.

By lowering costs to the individual and to society, sustainability improves every one's standard of living (SoL) and quality of life (QoL). The mind-set of sustainable decisions, while still revolutionary at present, is gaining. When it will reach its tipping point, expectations are that the breakthroughs will be extraordinary, as new doors of greatly superior rates of resource productivity will open that in turn will ensure novel, prosperous, and secure investments in innovative and sustainable living, and represent the core of a new powerful economic engine, all geared to the preservation of the environment, meant here not only as climate[96] and earth[97], but cultures and "places"[98], families and individuals[99].

---

94 energy efficiency and renewable energy system R&D is extremely broad in scope and range, for example in the biomedical field, from technologies to optimize battery usage and/or energy consumption by medical devices (e.g., hearing aids, dental hand-pieces, chairs, lights), to imaging technology (e.g., dental X-ray technology, magnetic resonance imaging systems), to radiation therapy equipment (e.g., accelerators for proton radiotherapy), to chair/bed-side information technology (e.g., computers and displays), to technologies to optimize energy consumption during production and delivery of radioisotopes and radiopharmaceuticals, to technologies to optimize large bioreactor technologies in pharmaceutical production, to monitor unit of research vital signs, diagnostics and medical care, thus decreasing transportation to specialized medical facilities, to improve technologies for production and assessment of biologicals, biofilms and anaerobic bacteria, to the development of instrumentation for dynamical analysis of lignocellulose processing, dueterated macromolecule resources, and medical device power sources (e.g., increased energy density, increased number of charge/discharge cycles before battery failure, solar cells, kinetic to electrical current conversion, fuel cells, and the like), to the crafting of circulatory support systems, and implantable rechargeable batteries, alternate power sources and transcutaneous energy transmission systems, the manufacture of compact implantable defibrillators, and the development of respiratory support systems, artificial lungs, ventilators, CPAP machines, implantable rechargeable batteries, and alternate power sources, to the development of increased capacity oxygen concentrator systems, more simply portable oxygen delivery systems with alternative energy sources, improved robotics and computer assisted surgery, alternative energy efficient separation techniques including membranes, adsorption, and alternatives to distillation, to bioenergy technologies for biomass conversion biorefinery innovation and integration for novel marine, plant, algal and microbial bioenergy sources, hydrogen production, to cellulosic ethanol, enzyme, recombinant DNA, genomic and metabolomic technology, to robust, sterilizable, on-line sensor or imaging technologies to quantify raw material usage and metabolites in industrial cell and tissue culture reactors, high throughput screening tools for optimizing and modeling the manufacturing conditions of biopharmaceuticals and tissue engineered products, *et cetera*.

95 e.g., starting at the beginning of the present decade, for instance, DuPont made investments directed specifically at reducing its greenhouse gas emissions by 72% compared the 1990 decade, and already have a net savings from that policy of over $2 billion.

96 it has been said that making sustainable decisions in the process of "... addressing climate change ...is the biggest job creation program there is..." (Paul Hawken of Smith & Hawken).

minimizing and recycling waste. More efficient use of pretty much anything is a step in the direction of sustainability, up to and including programs purchasing to transportation.

In brief, sustainability invariably leads to and drives substantial societal change: change in people's habits and behaviors, decisions, and decision-making paradigms.

The question remains as to how these changes are going to obtain.

Every program of change is associated with substantial costs: from development, to the training, to evaluation of outcomes, not including the overall administration of the program. The enactment of sustainable programs is not immune to these costs; however, the benefits outweigh the financial burden in most cases because sustainable programs, such energy efficiency and renewable

---

levels of radiation, and a conservative estimates suggest that the fallout resulted in additional cancer cases. The overall cost of the disaster may have been over US $200 bill

It is self-evident that sustainability is inexorably set to take a firmer hold in the next decade, and that this outcome will be optimal if – and only if – the fundamentals of sustainable decisions will be conveyed, taught and learned within the school system: from elementary to high school, from college to university, on to technical schools and continuing education throughout the lifespan of the individuals within a community.

Education is critical, and education in sustainability must be a priority locally and globally, lest a disarticulated effort ensues that yields chaotic, suboptimal and substandard outcomes, which together will not – cannot, because of their very disarticulated nature – lead to a substantial betterment of quality of life (QoL) and standard of living (SoL).

Our very first sustainable decision, as a society in this XXI Century, must be to mandate education in sustainability, and sustainable decisions, as the premier need and requirement of all social groups, in all nations, on all continents, across profession, trade and age. Humanity must respond to the urgency of correcting

---

97 for example, in theory, the wind could produce five times more electricity than the United States currently uses. Some of the best wind resources in the country are on farmland, especially in the plains states. However, the wind resource varies greatly from one location to another. Many states have developed wind resource maps and have been measuring the wind and collecting data that farmers could find useful for determining the wind potential on their land. While many people will benefit indirectly from the clean air and economic growth brought about by wind power development, farmers can benefit directly. Wind power can provide an important economic boost to farmers. Large wind turbines typically use less than half an acre of land, including access roads, so farmers can continue to plant crops and graze livestock right up to the base of the turbines.

The first heyday of wind power in America lasted from 1870 to 1930, when thousands of farmers used the wind to pump water and generate power. The second heyday is just beginning. Wind power is the fastest-growing energy source in the world, with annual average growth of 32 percent between 1998 and 2002. In the United States alone, nearly two billion dollars' worth of wind turbines are projected to come on line in 2003—enough to power 800,000 homes.

The U.S. Department of Energy's (DOE) "Wind Powering America" initiative has set a goal of producing five percent of the nation's electricity from wind by 2020. DOE projects meant to achieve this goal will provide $60 billion in capital investment to rural America, $1.2 billion in new income to farmers and rural landowners, and 80,000 new jobs during the next 20 years. Until recently, wind power was concentrated in California. Now it can be found in most states. Farming regions in the Midwest, Great Plains, and West have emerged as major growth areas. Wind power is growing partly as a result of technology improvements and cost reductions and partly in response to state and federal laws and incentives.

Some environmentalists and biologists, though, also argue that wind turbine are unsightly, and dangerous to migratory bird species, among others.

98 Cf., Maida CA. Ed. Sustainability and communities of place. In Studies in Environmental Anthropology and Ethnobiology (vol 5) R. Ellen Series Editor, Berghahn Books, New York, NY, 2007

99 this is precisely Scharmer's (2009) vision of the potential we all have, and must unleash to grow into the future as it emerges.

and reversing our current, common and widely disseminated unsustainable habits, self-satisfying needs, and immediate gratification.

"Is this or that *nice to have*, or is it *a need to have?*" – so goes the refrain that many parents teach their teenage children while imparting upon them the fundamentals of financial responsibility.

Well, sustainability is unquestionably *a need to have*, a must have, an urgent must have!

To obtain and to establish sustainability in our world locally and globally for our and future generations, we must develop in ourselves and in our children a sense *of* responsibility of sustainability – a sense of responsibility *for* sustainability. That can only arise as a complementary consequence of our acquiring a sense of ownership of our own world and our lives as we strive for quality of life (QoL) and standard of living (SoL) for all, and not just for ourselves: we are not here alone and in passing only, we are here as part of the family of all of the inhabitants of this planet, and we are here all as equals to prepare this planet for improved quality of life (QoL) and standard of living (SoL) for future generations. Case in point is the report by the National Oceanic and Atmospheric Administration entitled *Global Climate Change: Impacts in the United States*, which is still in its draft form at the time of this printing.

In other words, we must develop an increasing sense of ownership and responsibility for a sustainable world, as we develop and apply sustainable habits and decisions. These can only be acquired by learning about them, how to use them, and the extent to which we "make them ours". Education empowers us to make sustainable decisions.

In the realm of higher education, for example, the Association for the Advancement of Sustainability in Higher Education (AASHE) initiated a collaborative process among volunteer participants and reviewers from higher education institutions and associations, related nonprofit organizations, business, and governmental institutions[100]. The project is endorsed by the Higher Education Associations Sustainability Consortium (HEASC), and seeks to develop a campus sustainability rating system to rate and monitor – rather than rank[101] – the progress of individual institutions of higher learning in their concerted goal toward:

---

100 Cf., also /chronicle.com/weekly/v55/i40/40netzero.htm

101 The proposed rating system refers to a self-reporting system where levels of achievement (a "rating") are highlighted rather than the actual numerical score. In contrast, a ranking system typically implies a survey performed by a third party, with campuses ranked from best to worst according to a numerical score. A rating system offers a better way of promoting change, as institutions strive toward the highest level of achievement, rather than simply focusing on getting ahead of other institutions. With a ranking system an institution may wind up at the top just by virtue of being ahead of the rest – even if it's still far from achieving sustainability –

- achieving sustainability in campus,
- research projects toward improved sustainability, and
- teaching sustainability issues and decision-making to their student bodies.

At this printing, the instrument, tentatively called the Sustainability Tracking, Assessment, and Rating System (STARS), has gone through preliminary beta-testing and is in its final development phase.

In brief, STARS draws on concepts of sustainability embodied in the simultaneous consideration of environmental, economic, and equity issues in all sustainable decisions, and holds common goals of healthy environments, thriving communities, and meaningful livelihoods, while integrating democratic governance & education critical to sustainability. STARS offer a "roadmap" for individual campuses to move along the long way toward sustainability in each sector. It enables meaningful comparisons across and within institutions by providing benchmark for institution's progress over time.

In its structure, it is reminiscent of the logic model[102]: STARS imbeds creative incentives for continuous improvement. This is a fundamental goal of

---

while in a rating system the top classification could be empty for many years while schools work toward it. Advantages of a rating system include:

- it allows for more in depth questions - Campuses participating in a rating system are generally doing so in anticipation of receiving positive recognition, so would be more motivated to respond to more complex questions and a more thorough survey. A ranking system, in contrast, generally depends on institutions filling out a survey for a third party, which means the survey must be fairly easy to complete (less complex and thorough) so that institutions will respond.
- it provides a clear standard, while ranking creates a moving target - A rating system provides a clear "road map" for a campus to reach a benchmark level at any time. In contrast, a ranking system provides no clear target (a campus won't know in advance where it will end up in the rankings).
- it tends to be generally more transparent - Scoring and weighting are generally transparent in rating systems, as opposed to 3rd party ranking systems. Some rating systems may be 3rd party and less transparent (e.g., where a grade is assigned by an independent body).
- it emphasizes positive recognition - Rating systems give only positive recognition through levels of achievement, while ranking systems also provide negative recognition (being "bottom of the heap") and can generate bad feelings. Rating systems
- may lead to invidious competitions between schools closely ranked in order, which creates incentives to "game the system."
- it provides the opportunity to be self-funding - A rating system can be self-sustaining through a submission fee while a ranking system requires significant outside funding each time for the third party to perform its work.
- it favors more inclusiveness - A rating system offers beginner levels of achievement that give even "novice" schools something to work toward. In contrast, with a ranking system, only schools that expect to be in the top grouping would have an incentive to participate, since those not very far along would look bad.

102 Vide supra, Part I

STARS: to build stronger, more diverse campus sustainability communities, and to involve all sectors of campus, including sectors focused on social components of sustainability (diversity, community engagement, labor, health and well being, social responsibility, etc.) in sustainable decision-making for the betterment of the campus, its internal programmatic structure as well as its outreach to the surrounding community and the world. It utilizes a checklist of indicators similar to the Leadership in Energy and Environmental Design (LEED). This standardized checklist addresses two groups of indicators:

- Tier One indicators are "outcomes" oriented;
- Tier Two are "strategies" for achieving outcomes (e.g., program implementation)

Similar to LEED, STARS yields four levels of achievement (1-star, 2-stars, etc.), which are determined by point values corresponding to the indicators. This process of quantification[103] permits a numerical assessment of the criteria for achieving best sustainability practices for environmental stewardship and social responsibility commonly accepted in both higher education and the business world. It also permits assessment of progress of any given campus over time, and comparison across campuses. Of course, STARS, while an encouraging beginning, proffers neither a complete nor the sole approach to effect sustainability education in general, and in higher education institutions in particular.

In closing, it must be mentioned that several ongoing campus endeavors are noteworthy, and the following sample can serve as examples for future dissemination and expansion:

- Sustainable Environment Institute
- Harvard, Green Campus Loan Fund
- UCLA Climate Action Plan
- UC-wide Policy for Sustainable Practices
- Washington University in St. Louis, Living Building Challenge
- Ohlone Community College, San Francisco[104]

---

103 which is by no means universally applauded. Some argue against it on the grounds, for instance that it is simplistic, and does not permit satisfactory statistical analysis and inference of the data (e.g., acceptable sampling, vide supra)

104 the college recently opened a 135,000-square-foot, $58-million Center for Health Sciences that is essentially off the grid about half of the year. The structure draws heat and power from geothermal technology and photovoltaic panels.

- Cornell University, National Renewable Energy Laboratory[105]


## 4.3. EVIDENCE-BASED SUSTAINABLE DECISIONS

Participation of citizens in political, economic or social decisions is increasingly recognized as a precondition to foster sustainable development processes. Since spatial information is often important during planning and decision-making, participatory mapping gains in popularity. However, little attention has been paid to the fact that information must be presented in a useful way to reach city planners and policy makers. Above all, the importance of visualization tools to support collaboration, analytical reasoning, problem solving and decision-making in analyzing and planning processes has been underestimated (Pfeiffer et al, 2008).

In the context of "sustainable development", it is important to establish the attributes that are important to people's quality of life (QoL) because they help predict what changes in QoL people could result from future sustainable *vis à vis* unsustainable economic and environmental changes, societal improvements or deteriorations. In a now "classic study", about 200 adult subjects evaluated the relative importance of 22 different QoL attributes. Research shows that QoL attributes (or factors[106]) "healthy", "family", "environmental quality", "nature" and "safety" to be most important, while "recognition", "comfort", "status" and "spiritual life" were found to be least important. Further research established that expected changes in those QoL factors could derive from alterations in economic and environmental conditions, in addition to gender, income and age. In brief, QoL was found to be best conceptualized a multi-factorial construct: a meta-construct that may be useful for assessing the expected effects of future economic and environmental conditions (Vlek et al , 1998)

This meta-construct of QoL has become central and critical to sustainable evidence-based decision-making in health care, and across other fields. To conduct a basic sustainability analysis of health systems, and explore models for conceptualizing and creating sustainable organizations, based upon the

---

105 a division of the Department of Energy. The charge of this endeavor is in part to establish the National Center of Expertise on Net-Zero Carbon Campuses

106 the terminology of factors and clusters is probably more accurate, since such attributes are generally derived by procedures and protocols that are based statistically on factor analysis and cluster analysis (cf., Chiappelli, 2008; novapublishers.com/catalog/product_info.php? products_id=5937). These techniques yield information about variable interdependencies based on individual factor loadings. This methodology was spearheaded by Charles Spearman (1863-1945) and Raymond Cattell (1905 – 1998).

experiences of the environmental sciences and organizational theory, the role of information technologies in assisting health organizations become sustainable enterprises must be explored. Indeed, most health systems around the globe face dual challenges of increasing demands and diminishing resources, which are ultimately unsustainable, principally because health care is an open system that needs to be sufficiently adaptive to changes if it is to sustain. Information and communication technologies (i.e., IT and CT) are increasingly recognized as critical and crucial tools to enable any large and complex modern enterprise to model, measure and then manage business processes, including organizational simulation, electronic health record, and decision support. Formal sustainability analyses of health systems are necessary on a global scale to identify pressing challenges, and to explore innovative designs for improving health system policies, infrastructure and services (Coiera & Hovenga, 2007).

In a similar vein, the analytic hierarchy process (AHP) is a multi-criteria evaluation and decision support system that purports to incorporate multiple sustainability criteria, weighted strategically responsive to local public policy priorities and community-specific situations and values, while gauging and directing desirable future courses of development. The decision support system uses a Geographic Information Systems (GIS), which facilitates an assessment of urban form with multiple indicators of sustainability as spatial criteria thematically. The resultant land-use sustainability scores indicate, on the ratio-scale of AHP, whether or not a desirable urban form is likely in the long run, and if so, to what degree. The two alternative modes of synthesis in AHP-ideal and distributive-provide assessments of a land development plan incrementally (short-term) and citywide pattern comprehensively (long-term), respectively. Thus, the spatial decision support system facilitates proactive and collective public policy determination of land resource for future sustainable urban development (Banai, 2005). This approach, particularly relevant in the assessment of land resource sustainability for urban development, points as an example for a model generalizable across many others, or all domains pertinent to sustainability, and characterizes the problem of decision-making with multiplicity and uncertainty.

In this context, the Geographic Information Systems (GIS) has a strong potential to become an information technology enabling groups of people to participate in decisions shaping their communities and promoting sustainable use of natural resources, because it will encourage participation in the context of planning and decision making. Participatory GIS (PGIS) offers tools that can be used to empower citizens in making decisions about their communities and resources (Jankowski, 2008).

A decision support system prototype aids in the assessment of incremental land development plan proposals put forth within the long-term community priority of a sustainable growth.
Examples include, but are not limited to:

- cities, towns and villages have become increasingly dependent on motorized transport and a car-based land-use pattern, which has led to a series of unintended consequences (e.g., a lack of regular exercise, the decline of local communities and excessive greenhouse gas emissions with huge long-term impacts on health and well-being). Official policies are seeking new policies – that will lend themselves to testing and evaluation with the Ex-GRADE[107] - to change the trend, with much rhetoric about 'sustainable development' and 'sustainable communities'. Yet many of the decision processes that control change in the built environment have not caught up with the new agenda, and further assessments are needed with a particular focus on environmental impact analysis and health impact research. Additional studies are needed to examine the relative strengths and weaknesses of the tools used to examine the degree to which they are systematic in their approach to health and sustainability, and include all those who have a legitimate interest in the outcomes (e.g., the Spectrum appraisal protocol[108]) (Barton & Grant, 2008).

- managing natural resources in a sustainable way is a difficult and arduous task, due to uncertainties, dynamics and conflicting objectives (ecological, social, and economical). A stochastic viability approach can consider a discrete-time control dynamic model with uncertainties[109], representing a bioeconomic system. The sustainability of this system should not be described by a set of constraints, defined in practice by indicators - namely, state, control and uncertainty functions - together with thresholds. This would ensure identifying decision rules such that a set of constraints, representing various objectives with maximal probability (de Lara & Martinet, 2008).

---

107 vide supra, Part II

108 Spectrum appraisal technique is based on, and derives from the logical model, and is a practical process that facilitates consensus-building and creativity in decision-making. This protocol is reportedly effective to help ensure a healthier, more sustainable urban environment, and for overall for sustainability and health

109 cf., probability-based decision-making – vide supra, Part I

- an interactive mental map tool could merge socio-economic and geospatial data on infrastructure, local perceptions, coping and adaptation strategies with remote sensing data and modern technology of map making. This interactive mapping tool could provide for insights into different locally-constructed realities and facilitated the communication of results to the wider public and respective policy makers, prove useful in visualizing information and promoting participatory decision-making processes, and spatially and temporally assess key health themes such as availability of, and accessibility to, existing health care services, breeding sites of disease vectors, collection and storage of water, waste disposal, location of public toilets or defecation sites (Pfeiffer et al, 2008).

- toward global and integrated approaches to water resources management, both from the quantitative and the qualitative point of view, water quality management is a major issue for sustainable development and a mandatory task with respect to the implementation of the European Water Framework Directive as well as the Swiss legislation, for example. Data modeling to develop relational databases and subsequent geographic information system (GIS)-based water management instruments are a rather recent and not widespread are now available, and guidelines for data modeling along with the EU Water Framework Directive is an important milestone in this area. Improving overall water quality requires better and more easily accessible data, but also the possibility to link data to simulation models. Together, these models ought to be expanded and generalized to be used in the derivation of indicators that will in turn support decision-making processes (Soutter et al, 2008).

- the creation of an informed policy decision-making process grounded in the best available information at a national level to help ensure that decisions are financially sustainable. Any vaccine purchasing mechanisms should address the following essential points: 1) prioritization of cost-saving interventions; 2) flexible participation; 3) sufficient support to confront in-country challenges for managing vaccine procurement mechanisms[110] (e.g., anti H1N1/A; anti Human papillomavirus; anti-Hepatitis C virus); 4) a definite time-line for country ownership of vaccine purchases; 5) accuracy of vaccine demand forecasting; 6) maintenance of vaccine supply chains; and 7) well-functioning surveillance and regulatory bodies (Andrus et al, 2008).

---

110 cf., related work by our group: Chiappelli et al, 2008; Kangueane et al, 2008; Shapshak et al, 2008, 2009

- practical and theoretically sound methods for analyzing innovative environmental technologies are needed to inform public and private decisions regarding research and development, risk management, and stakeholder communication. By integrating scientific assessments with a characterization of values, multicriteria decision analysis (MCDA) supports the ranking of alternative technology pathways on the basis of technical, financial, and social concerns (Borsuk et al, 2008).

- development and better use of sustainability relevant knowledge is key, and that this requires capacity building globally, and especially in the less developed regions of the world. Also essential is stronger integration of high-quality knowledge creation and technology--and policy--development, including, importantly, the creation of centers of excellence in developing regions which effectively use and produce applications-directed high quality research and bring it to bear on decision making and practices related to environmental change and sustainable management of natural resources. Centers of excellence are a necessary first step for bottom-up societal transformation towards sustainability, and such centers must help design innovative ways to assess and place value on ecosystem services (Nobre et al, 2008).

- delivery of novel developments in comparative risk analysis, strategic risk analysis, weight of evidence frameworks, and participative decision making must take account of organizational capabilities in risk management and the institutional culture that implements decision on risk[111]. To manage risk knowledge within organizations, and to emphasize the use of core criteria for effective risk-based decisions by reference to decision process, implementation and the security of strategic added value are critical (Pollard et al, 2008).

- the ELECTRE III decision-aid method in the context of choosing a sustainable demolition waste management strategy for a case study in the city of Lyon, France. This choice of waste management strategy takes into consideration the sustainable development objectives, economic aspects, environmental consequences, and social issues. Nine alternatives for demolition waste management were compared with the aid of eight criteria, taking into account energy consumption, depletion of abiotic resources, global warming, dispersion of dangerous substances in the environment, economic activity, employment, and quality of life of the local population. The case study concerned the demolition of 25

---

111 *vedi supra*, Part I

buildings of an old military camp. Each alternative was illustrated with different waste treatments, such as material recovery, recycling, landfilling, and energy recovery. The recommended solution for sustainable demolition waste management for the case study was reported to be a selective deconstruction of each building with local material recovery in road engineering of inert wastes, local energy recovery of wood wastes, and specific treatments for hazardous wastes (Roussat et al, 2009).

In closing, general systems theory emphasizes the way in which organized systems (human and non-human) respond in an adaptive way to cope with significant changes in their external environments so as to maintain their basic structures intact. Systems theory models of decision-making in human groups and organizations emphasize their interaction with "outside" actors and organizations and concentrate on identifying the particular elements in the environment of the group or organization that significantly affect the outcomes of its decision-making.

A theoretical model of how public policy decisions are (or perhaps ought to be) taken suggests that all possible options or approaches to solving the problem under study must be listed, and identified, and the costs and benefits of each option are assessed and compared with each other. The option that promises to yield the greatest net benefit selected. The main problem with such rational-comprehensive approaches is that they often are very costly in terms of time and resources that must be devoted to gathering the relevant information. The costs and benefits of the various options are uncertain and difficult to quantify for rigorous comparison. The costs of undertaking rational-comprehensive decision-making may themselves exceed the benefits to be gained in improved quality of decisions[112].

Where formal organizations are the setting in which decisions are made, the particular decisions or policies chosen by decision-makers can often be explained through reference to the organization's particular structure and procedural rules. Such explanations typically involve looking at the distribution of responsibilities among organizational sub-units, the activities of committees and ad hoc coordinating groups, meeting schedules, rules of order etc. The notion of fixed-in-

---

112 hence, ill-advised from the perspective of CER – *vide supra*, Part II

advance standard operating procedures (SOPs) typically plays an important role in such explanations of individual decisions made[113].

Due to the immense volumes of medical data[114], and research results[115], the architecture of the future health care decision support systems focus more on

113 hence, not really following the logic model or the uncertainty model (vide supra, Part II), and therefore not truly optimal as a decision-making tool in this context.

114 To paraphrase a recent statement by the National Institutes of Health (NIH), recent advances in science and technology areas such as cancer biology, cell biology, molecular biology, systems biology, biomarkers, combinatorial chemistry, genomics, tissue engineering, bioinformatics and high throughput screening technology provide unprecedented opportunities for discovery of new disease prevention/intervention/treatment entities and understanding of both the useful and potential adverse biological effects of environmental agents and chemicals. It is expected that research focused on the discovery and validation of new targets and agents that affect these targets will result in new chemical and biological agents with the potential for clinical benefit, and will identify how exposures to these and other substances in the home and workplace may be contributing to or causing injury or disease. Before new agents can be assessed and used in humans, pre-clinical safety assessments must be conducted. Similar safety assessments should also be made prior to exposure of the public to new chemicals and products introduced into the workplace, home, foods, water, or air. Current practices and procedures for safety assessments are costly, time consuming and utilize large amounts of compound and large numbers of animals. There are enormous potential benefits to applying advances in science and technology to develop new safety assessment tools and integrated strategies that can be used to evaluate whether and how new agents and other chemical entities perturb key toxicity pathways that can lead or contribute to disease and injury. Such tools and strategies can be used to quickly assess large numbers of compounds, as well as analogs in a chemical series

Recent advances in all branches of medical science, the NIH statement added, provide new insight into the underlying mechanisms in a variety of diseases and suggest new targets and approaches to therapy. Drug discovery can now be focused on targeting key regulatory pathways or specific macromolecules relevant to the disease state. For example, key growth regulatory pathways and mutations in genes predisposing for specific disease states are being identified at an increasing rate using new techniques and bioinformatics tools. New technologies in chemistry that allow facile synthesis of millions of new chemicals and high resolution structures of important target proteins are becoming available. These advances taken together and coupled with high throughput screening methods allow for the identification of large numbers of agents that could be considered for clinical evaluation. Translation of these new technological discoveries and innovations into clinical benefit through these newly discovered agents is essential; however, the later stages in this drug development process are lengthy and costly. Obviously, new methods are needed to decide which of the multitude of new agents should ultimately move forward to clinical trials. Similarly, it is important to understand the potential adverse health effects that may result from human exposure to the thousands of chemicals in the home, workplace, and environment, and whether these substances may be contributing to or causing human diseases or injuries.

Investigations focusing on the toxicity of potential cancer, AIDS or other drugs or biologicals designed to reduce the incidence or severity of disease to healthy organs in intact experimental animals are, the NIH stipulates,  the final steps in the preclinical stages of new drug development. Data generated from these studies on each new drug are evaluated in light of potential human toxicity and form a major portion of the information required by the Food and Drug Administration (FDA) for an Investigational New Drug (IND) application. Preclinical toxicology studies are generally conducted in two animal species with the following objectives: to define the Maximum Tolerated Dose (MTD), Dose Limiting Toxicities (DLTs), schedule-dependency of toxicity, reversibility of adverse effects, and a safe clinical Starting Dose (SD). The animal studies required to obtain such information for an IND application have significant limitations, both in terms of cost and time requirements as well as prediction of problems to be encountered when agents are administered to humans. For example, since animal studies are very expensive and time-consuming, it is generally impractical to evaluate numerous analogs of a chemical series or large numbers of possible candidates from a high throughput screening program. Another concern is the lack of information gained from animal toxicology studies in regard to molecular mechanisms for observed toxicities. It cannot be determined if toxicities of new agents designed to attack a key molecular target are related to actions of inhibition of that target or to other unknown aspects of the drug's action in various organs.

In addition to assays that will be important to drug development and testing, the NIH predicts that these scientific advances provide opportunities to develop new and innovative tests to determine the safety or toxicity of environmental chemicals. The National Institute of Environmental Health Sciences (NIEHS) has been directed by Congress to develop and validate alternatives for acute and chronic toxicity testing that will reduce or eliminate the use of animals. In addition, the Interagency Coordinating Committee on the Validation of Alternative Methods (ICCVAM) and the National Toxicology Program (NTP) Interagency Center for the Validation of Alternative Toxicological Methods (NICEATM) indicated in their five year plan (2008-2012) that the development and validation of alternative tests for ocular, dermal, reproductive and developmental toxicity, carcinogenicity, immunotoxicity, as well as biologics, pyrogen and endocrine disruptor testing and acute and chronic toxicity tests were all high priority needs.

The mission of the NTP, an interagency program located at NIEHS, is to evaluate agents of public health concern by developing and applying tools of modern toxicology and molecular biology. Currently, the NTP tests chemicals of environmental or occupational concern using study designs similar to that used in preclinical toxicology studies, including 30- and 90-day toxicity studies, two-year bioassay to determine the chronic toxicity and carcinogenic potential of chemicals, two-generation studies to determine reproductive toxicity and in utero exposure to determine developmental toxicity. The goal of the NTP is to develop new and novel alternative toxicity tests that could replace or reduce the use of animals in toxicity testing and to provide mechanistic information on a potentially hazardous environmental agent that would aid in intervention/prevention efforts.

The NTP has recently partnered with the National Human Genome Research Institute's NIH Chemical Genomics Center and the U.S. Environmental Protection Agency's National Center for Computational Toxicology to establish a HTS program to screen for mechanistic targets active within cellular pathways critical to carcinogenicity, reproductive and developmental toxicity, genotoxicity, neurotoxicity, and immunotoxicity. The U.S. EPA is also developing a two tiered approach for the identification of endocrine disrupting chemicals. Thus, there is interest and commitment across the NIH and U.S. EPA to be proactive in stimulating the reduction of animals in toxicity testing and the development of new approaches including in vitro and computational models to identify cellular targets that would be predictive of tissue injury and cancer (e.g., biomarkers) (cf., Oluwadara & Chiappelli, 2009).

New technologies to improve toxicology from an observation-based to a mechanism-based science are emerging, but as yet none has been validated and accepted for common use. These new technologies will be highly valuable when combined with other approaches to develop a total toxicological profile of specific organ toxicity and molecular mechanisms responsible for this toxicity.

115  A critical review is provided of a number of extrapolation issues that arise in undertaking an ecological risk assessment: acute versus chronic exposure regime; radiation quality including relative biological effectiveness and radiation weighting factors; biological effects from an individual to a population level, including radiosensitivity and lifestyle variations throughout the life cycle; single radionuclide versus multi-contaminants. The specificities of the environmental situations of interest (mainly chronic low-level exposure regimes) emphasize the importance of

inter-operability than on integration. With the raising need for the creation of unified knowledge base, the federated approach to distributed data warehouses (DWH) is getting increasing attention as a sustainable, appropriate and legitimate solution. Further, we present a federated DWH enables the interoperability between heterogeneous and distributed medical system and response mechanism and facilitates evidence-based medicine[116] (Stolba et al, 2007).

DWH is a working model of human IT. As healthcare enterprises seek to move towards an integrated, sustainable healthcare delivery model an IT-enabled or e-Healthcare strategy ought to be established to identify the critical success factors influencing the effectiveness of such an approach. The performance of an e-Healthcare strategy in India was based on assessment criteria used to measure effectiveness were increasing reach and reducing cost of healthcare delivery. Nevertheless, the importance of the human value should not be diminished, and the focus should not be on the IT tools and biomedical engineering technologies as is most often the case. Instead the nontechnology factors such as healthcare provider and consumer mindsets should be addressed to increase acceptance of, and enhance the effectiveness of, sustainable e-Healthcare services (Taneja, 2007).

---

reproductive parameters governing the demography of the population within a given ecosystem and, as a consequence, the structure and functioning of that ecosystem (Garnier-Laplace, et al, 2004).

116 Vide supra

# Chapter 5

# CONCLUSION

"...Cognitive research shows that approximately 95% of what we do is unconscious and the brain is constantly working to free up its 5% of conscious reserves by converting new behaviors into unconscious habit as quickly as possible..." (Sharp, 2009; Bargh & Chartrand, 1999).

The goal of sustainable use is indefinite use of the planet by humankind. This objective, in turn, requires that the planet's ecological life support system, consisting of natural capital and ecosystem services, remains healthy for an indefinite period. Achieving sustainability will require a new view of the responsibilities of professionals, such as ecotoxicologists, to ensure a healthy ecological life support system. Because both human society and natural systems are complex and multivariate, a high degree of uncertainty will remain. Therefore, sound judgment will be needed in determining what, if any, precautionary measures should be taken until more robust information has been gathered. The role of decision-makers in the quest for sustainable use of the planet is varied, and includes:

- shifting goals and endpoints from an absence of harm to persuasive evidence of health;
- increasing both temporal and spatial scales of ecotoxicological studies;
- achieving a critical mass of qualified personnel;
- including demographic change in sustainable decision-making analysis and judgment;
- deciding upon and developing new ecological thresholds;

- being prepared for environmental unexpected and uncharted phenomena and outcomes;
- focusing on design for a quality environment for this and future generations;
- developing a set of biosphere services that will serve as starting point (e.g., PIC/PO question) and as endpoints in sustainable decision-making studies,
- being prepared for serious events that might destabilize the biosphere and require major adjustments in the process of adaptation.

Both sustainable use of the planet and the field of sustainable decision-making are rapidly developing fields that are mostly evolving in isolation from each other. To be successful, they must co-evolve (Cairns, 2002). This effort must address everything from governance structures and decision-making processes, change management, finance and accounting practices, hidden institutional drivers and compartmentalization, engagement, capacity building, systems thinking and leadership. New education and governance models and decision-making processes must be created to enable effective societal engagement in the sustainability enterprise. A distributed model of ownership, accountability, and control must coordinate finance, human resources, facilities, development, government and community relations, and academics into a shared state of responsibility and collaboration.

Despite our own individual best efforts, passion, and commitment, most of us professionals in the field, are quickly overburdened, and are without the skills, structure, or staffing level to achieve the necessary broad-reaching cross-disciplinary and multi-disciplinary institutional engagement and transformation. In fact, it is our very organizations and their structural organization that need to make a sizable investment in change and functional progress toward sustainability.

We must change our world view, and adapt our *modus cogitandi* and *modus vivendi* fundamentally, drastically, completely away from the "traditional" (=pre-industrial revolution), and the "industrial" (=post industrial revolution to present) frame of mind and mode of action, as Sharmer (2009) refers to, toward a new frontier: that of a sustainable environment. Every step of the way in this transformation, and every step that will cement us in this transformed state of mind, must and will depend on our abilities to be effective sustainable evidence-based decision-makers for our immediate benefit and for the benefit of future generations, in all domains of human endeavors, from the political, financial, human resource, technological, art and art education[117], and otherwise.

Sustainable decisions are destined to change mindful opinions, and direct actions. Decisions arise from a process, whose closure brings about the onset of this renewal. The process of making sustainable decisions is complex, and can certainly not be rendered as simplistically as the economist Jacob Viner[118] suggested eight decades ago: "(decision making)... *is not under the constant and detailed guidance of careful and accurate hedonic calculations, but is the product of an unstable and unrational complex of reflex actions, impulses, instincts, habits, customs, fashion, and hysteria...*".

Rather, sustainable decisions are a set of modalities that rests on firm and varied theoretical foundations, that range from uncertainty and odds to rationality and logic, and that must be grounded on the best available evidence for the desired outcome as well as for maximizing benefits and minimizing risks. In that light, this monograph has discussed the process of sustainable evidence-based decision-making as one driven to obtain the best available evidence to ensure and to secure maximizing benefits and minimizing riskas to QoL and to SoL for this generations and the generations of our children.

---

117 in this context, it must be emphasized that museums are indispensable to civil society, especially in an era in which museums often are reduced to cultural businesses or "edu-tainment" sites. Museum leaders must be empowered with a different set of criteria for evaluating the success of their museums, proposing a set of sustainable values that can help museums preserve themselves and advance their social mission in hard times-and help them thrive when times improve (Holo & Alvarez, 2009).

118 Jacob Viner (3 May 1892 – 12 September 1970). Academician at University of Chicago, Stanford, Yale, Ecole des Hautes Etudes, Geneva Switzerland, and Princeton University. During the inter-war period, he trained several renown economists, including Milton Friedman (31 July 1912 – 16 November 2006), Nobel Laureate economist.

# ABOUT THE AUTHOR

Professor Chiappelli obtained his undergraduate, graduate (Ph.D., 1986), and post-doctoral training at UCLA. Indeed, he has been continuously at UCLA since 1972. Professor Chiappelli was recruited by the School of Dentistry to establish a curriculum in Evidence-Based Dentistry, which he still teaches to undergraduate pre-dental students, to dental students, to graduate students (M.S. and Ph.D.), and to Residents, post-doctoral fellows and international visiting scholars. He also teaches evidence-based decision-making in dentistry to dentists in the community in the continuing education program nationally and internationally. He is a Champion for the American Dental Association (ADA) in Evidence-Based Dentistry, an Evidence Reviewer for ADA, and was nominated for the ADA Gold Medal for excellence for his work in evidence-based research and decision-making. He sits on the Council of the American Association for the Advancement of Science-Pacific Division (AAAS-PD), and was nominated for membership in the US Division of the Club of Rome, as well as the Federal Committee on Comparative Effectiveness Research. As a Fullbright Specialist, he has extensive interactions and collaborative endeavors with Brazil, Nigeria, the Philippines, and other emerging and developing societies, as well as with Western Europe, Autralia and Canada. He has served as Chair of the academic committee for sustainability at UCLA, and on the UCLA Chancellor's Sustainability committee. He is a professor in the Divisions of Oral Biology & Medicine, and Associated Clinical Specialties (joint). His Manual for evidence-based research in the health sciences (Nova Publisher, 2008) is available through this publishing house.

# REFERENCES

Andrus JK, Sherris J, Fitzsimmons JW, Kane MA, Aguado MT. Introduction of human papillomavirus vaccines into developing countries - international strategies for funding and procurement. *Vaccine.* 2008 26S:K87-92

Banai R. Land resource sustainability for urban development: spatial decision support system prototype. *Environ Manage.* 2005 36:282-96

Banning M. A review of clinical decision-making: models and current research. *J Clin Nursing,* 2007, 17:187-95.

Bargh J, Chartrand T. The unbearable automaticity of being. *American Psychol* 1999 54:462–79.

Barton H, Grant M. Testing time for sustainability and health: striving for inclusive rationality in project appraisal. *J R Soc Promot Health.* 2008 128:130-9.

Bates DW, Larizgoitia I, Prasopa-Plaizier N, Jha AK. Global priorities for unit of research safety research: Research Priority Setting Working Group of the WHO World Alliance for Unit of research Safety. *BMJ.* 2009 338:b1775.

Bauer JG, Spackman S, Chiappelli F, Prolo P, Stevenson RG. Making Clinical Decisions using a Comon & practical Guideline. *Calif Dent Assoc J,* 2006 34:519-28.

Borsuk ME, Maurer M, Lienert J, Larsen TA. Charting a path for innovative toilet technology using multicriteria decision analysis. *Environ Sci Technol.* 2008 42:1855-62.

Cairns J Jr. Ecotoxicology and sustainable use of the planet. *Toxicol Ind Health.* 2002 18:162-70

Chiappelli F, Prolo P, Cajulis OS. Evidence-Based Research in Complementary and Alternative Medicine I. *Evidence-Based Complementary and Alternative Medicine* 2005 2:453-8.

Chiappelli F, Prolo P, Rosenblum M, Edgeron M, Cajulis OS. Evidence-Based Research in Complementary and Alternative Medicine II: The Process of Evidence-Based Research. *Evidence-Based Comp Alt Med.* 2006a 3:3-12.

Chiappelli F, Manfrini E, Edgerton M, Rosenblum M, Kristine D. Cajulis KD, Prolo P. Clinical Evidence and Evidence-Based Dental Treatment of Special Populations: Patients with Alzheimer's Disease. *California Dental Association Journal*, 2006b 34:439-47

Chiappelli F, Shapshak P, Commins D, Singer E, Kangueane P, Minagar A, Oluwadara O, Prolo P, Pellionisz AJ. Molecular Epigenetics, Chromatin, and NeuroAIDS/HIV: Immunopathological Implications. *Bioinformation* 2008, 3:47-52.

Chiappelli F, Cajulis OS. Transitioning Toward Evidence-Based Research in the Health Sciences for the XXI Century. *Evid Based Compl Alt Med* 2008 5:123-8.

Chiappelli F, Cajulis OS. The logic model in evidence-based clinical decision-making in dental practice. *J Evid Based Dent Pract* 2009 (In Press).

Chiappelli F, Cajulis O, Newman M. Comparative Effectiveness Research in Evidence-Based Dental Practice. *J Evid Based Dent Pract* 2009a 9:57-8.

Chiappelli F. Brant XMC, Oluwadara OO, Neagos N, Ramchandani MH. (Eds.) Understanding Evidence-Based Practice: *Toward Optimizing Clinical Outcomes.* Springer 2009b.

Chiappelli F, Cajulis OC, Oluwadara O, Ramchandani MH. Evidence-Based Based Decision Making - Implications for Clinical Dentistry. In F. Columbus, Ed. *Clinical Dentistry: Diagnostic, Preventive, and Restorative Services.* NovaScience Hauppauge NY 2009c

Coiera E, Hovenga EJ. *Building a sustainable health system.* Yearbook Med Inform. 2007 11-8.

CRD – Critical Review Dissemination. Systematic Reviews. York University Press, York GB, 2009

Damasio AR, Tranel D, Damasio H. *Somatic markers and the guidance of behavior: theory and preliminary testing.* In Levin HS, Eisenberg HM, Benton AL, Eds., Frontal Lobe Function and Dysfunction. Oxford University Press, New York, 1991.

De Lara M, Martinet V. Multi-criteria dynamic decision under uncertainty: A stochastic viability analysis and an application to sustainable fishery management. *Math Biosci.* 2008 Nov 24. Epub

Engel-Cox J, Van Houten B, Phelps J, Rose S. Conceptual model of comprehensive research metrics for improved human health and environment. Cien Saude Colet. 2009, 14:519-31

Etzioni A. Normative-Affective Factors: Towards a New Decision-Making Model. *J Economic Psychol*, 1988 9:125-50.

Forrest J, Miller SA. Enhancing your practice through evidence-based decision making. *J Evid Base Dent Pract*. 2001. 1:51-7.

Forrest JL, Miller SA, Overman PR, Newman MG. (Eds.) *Evidence-based decision making: A translational guide for dental professionals.* Lippincott, Williams & Wilkins, Philadelphia, PA. 2008

French JRP, Rodgers W, Cobb S. *Adjustment as person-environment fit.* In GV Coelho, DA Hamburg and JE Adams, Eds. Coping and Adaptation. Chapter 11. Basic Books, Inc, Pub. New York, 1974.

Garnier-Laplace J, Gilek M, Sundell-Bergman S, Larsson CM. Assessing ecological effects of radionuclides: data gaps and extrapolation issues. *J Radiol Prot*. 2004 24:A139-55.

Garber AM, Tunis SR. Does comparative-effectiveness research threaten personalized medicine? N Engl J Med. 2009 360:1925-7. Glenn AL, Raine A, Schug RA. The neural correlates of moral decision-making in Psychopathy. *Molecul Psychiat* 2009, 14:5–6;

Gilbert TT, Taylor JS. How to evaluate and implement clinical policies. *Fam Pract Manag* 1999 6:28-33.

GRADE Working Group. Grading quality of evidence and strength of recommendation. *BMJ* 2004, 328:1-8

Green DP, Shapiro I. *Pathologies of Rational Choice Theory: A Critique of Applications in Political Science.* Yale University Press, 1994.

Guyatt GH, Oxman AD, Kunz R, Falck-Ytter Y, Vist GE, Liberati A, Schünemann HJ; GRADE Working Group. Going from evidence to recommendations. *BMJ* 2008 336:1049-51.

Hastings BS & Madaus G. *Handbook of formative and summative evaluation of student learning.* McGraw-Hill, New York NY, 1971

Holo S, Alvarez MT. *Beyond the Turnstile: Making the Case for Museums and Sustainable Values.* AltaMira Press, Lanham, MD, 2009 216pp.

Howden SM, Soussana JF, Tubiello FN, Chhetri N, Dunlop M, Meinke H. *Proc Natl Acad Sci U S A.* 2007 104:19691-6.

Jankowski P. Towards participatory geographic information systems for community-based environmental decision making. *J Environ Manage*. 2008 Jun 10. Epub

Kangueane P, Kayathri R, Kishore Sakharkar M, Flower DR, Sadler K, Chiappelli F, Segal DM, Shapshak P. Designing HIV Gp120 Peptide Vaccines: Rhetoric or Reality For NeuroAids. Chapter 9. *In The Spectrum of Neuro-AIDS*

*Disorders: Pathophysiology, Diagnosis, and Treatment.* K Goodkin, P Shapshak & Verma A, Eds. ASM Press, 2008

Kerckhoff AC, Davis KE. Value consensus and need complementarity in mate selection, *Am Sociol Rev,* 1962, 27:295-303

Kung J, Chiappelli F, Cajulis OS, Maida M, Avezova A, Kossan G, Chew L. From Systematic Reviews to Clinical Recommendations for Evidence-Based Health Care: Validation of Revised Assessment of Multiple Systematic Reviews (R-AMSTAR) for Grading of Clinical Relevance. *The Open Dentistry Journal* 2009 (In Press).

Kunst-Wilson WR, Zajonc RB. Affective discrimination of stimuli that cannot be recognized. *Science,* 1980, 207:557-8.

Lee D. Game theory and neural basis of social decision making. *Nat Neurosci.* 2008 11: 404–9.

Lin E-N, Zito R, Taylor MAP. A Review Of Travel-Time Prediction In Transport And Logistics. *Proc Eastern Asia Soc Transportation Studies* 2005, 5:1433-448.

Littell JH, Corcoran J, Pillai V (2008) *Systematic reviews and meta-analysis.* Oxford Univeristy Press, New York, NY. pp. 220.

Maida CA. Ed. Sustainability and communities of place. *In Studies in Environmental Anthropology and Ethnobiology* (vol 5) R. Ellen Series Editor, Berghahn Books, New York, NY, 2007

Mayeske GW & Lambur MT. *How to Design Better Programs: A Staff Centered Stakeholder Approach to Program Logic Modeling.* The Program Design Institute, Crofton MD 2001

Moradi DR, Moy PK, Chiappelli F. Evidence-based Research in Alternative Protocols to Dental Implantology: A Closer Look at Publication Bias. *CDA J* 2006 34:877-86.

Muller P & Insua DR. Issues in Bayesian Analysis of Neural Network Models. *Neural Computation* 1995, 10:571–92.

Nieri M, Clauser C, Pagliaro U, PiniPrato G. Individual unit of research data: A criterion in grading articles dealing with therapy outcomes. *J Evid Base Dent* 2003 3:122-6.

Nobre CA, Lahsen M, Ometto JP. Global environmental change research: empowering developing countries. *An Acad Bras Cienc.* 2008 80:523-9.

Oluwadara OO, Chiappelli F. Biomarkers for Early Detection of High Risk Cancers: From Gliomas to Nasopharyngeal Carcinoma. *Bioinformation* 2009 3:332-9.

Oman KS, Duran C, Fink R Evidence-based policy and procedures: an algorithm for success. *J Nurs Adm* 2008 38:47-51.

O'Neill ES, Dluhy NC, Chun E. Modelling novice clinical reasoning for a computerised decision support system. *J Advan Nursing* 2005, 49:68–77.

Payne JW. Contingent decision behavior. *Psychol Bull,* 1982, 80:439-53.

Pfeiffer C, Glaser S, Vencatesan J, Schliermann-Kraus E, Drescher A, Glaser R. Facilitating participatory multilevel decision-making by using interactive mental maps. *Geospat Health.* 2008 3:103-12

Pollard SJ, Davies GJ, Coley F, Lemon M. Better environmental decision making - recent progress and future trends. *Sci Total Environ.* 2008 400:20-31.

Reeves A, Chiappelli F, Cajulis OS. Evidence-based recommendations for the use of sealants. *Calif Dent Assoc J* 2006 34:540-6

Roussat N, Dujet C, Méhu J. Choosing a sustainable demolition waste management strategy using multicriteria decision analysis. *Waste Manag.* 2009 29:12-20.

Sanfey AG, Chang LJ. *Multiple systems in decision-making.* Ann N Y Acad Sci. 2008 1128:53-62.

Sawyer AG. Repetition, cognitive responses and persuasion. In RE Petty, TM Ostrom & TC Brock, Eds, *Cognitive responses in persuasion.* Hillsdale, NJ: Erlbaum, 1981.

Scharmer CO. Theory U. Berret-Koehler Publishers, Inc. San Francisco, CA 2009.

Schram SF, Caterino B. Eds. Making Political Science Matter: *Debating Knowledge, Research, and Method.* New York and London: New York University Press. 2006

Shapshak P, Chiappelli F, Commins D, Singer E, Levine AJ, Kangueane P, Somboonwit C, Minagar A, Pellionisz AJ. Molecular Epigenetics, Chromatin, and NeuroAIDS/HIV. Translational Implications. *Bioinformation* 2008, 3:53-7.

Shapshak P, Somboonwit C, Drumright LN, Frost SSDW Commins D, Tellinghuisen TL, Scott WK, Duncan R, McCoy C, Page JB, Giunta B, Fernandez F, Singer E, Levine A, Minagar A, Oluwadara O, Kotila T, Chiappelli F, Sinnott JT. Molecular and Contextual Markers of Hepatitis C Virus and Drug Use. *Mol Diag Ther* 2009 13:153-79.

Shapshak P, Chiappelli F, Somboonwit C, Sinnott J. Containing the influenza pandemic of 2009: lessons and implications. *Mol Diag Ther* 2009 (In Press).

Sharp, L. 2002. Greening campuses: the road from little victories to systemic transformation. *International Journal of Sustainability in Higher Education* 3(2):128–145.

Sharp L. Higher education: the quest for the sustainable campus. Sustainability: Science, *Practice, & Policy* 2009 5:1-8.

Shea BJ, Bouter LM, Peterson J, Boers M, Andersson N, Ortiz Z, Ramsay T, Bai A, Shukla VK, Grimshaw JM External validation of a measurement tool to assess systematic reviews (AMSTAR). *PLoS ONE* 2007a 2:e1350

Shea BJ, Grimshaw JM, Wells GA, Boers M, Andersson N, Hamel C, Porter AC, Tugwell P, Moher D, Bouter LM Development of AMSTAR: a measurement tool to assess the methodological quality of systematic reviews. *BMC Med Res Methodol* 2007b 7:10

Sherif M, Taub D, Hovland CI. Assimilation and contrast effects of anchoring stimuli on judgements. *J Exp Psychol,* 1958, 55:150-5.

Simon HA. *Models of bounded rationality.* (three volumes). Cambridge, Massachusetts: MIT Press, 1982.

Soutter M, Alexandrescu M, Schenk C, Drobot R. Adapting a geographical information system-based water resource management to the needs of the Romanian water authorities. *Environ Sci Pollut Res Int.* 2008 Nov 8. epub

Stolba N, Nguyen TM, Tjoa AM. Towards sustainable decision-support system facilitating EBM. *Conf Proc IEEE Eng Med Biol Soc.* 2007:4355-8

Stroup DF, Berlin JA, Morton SC, Olkin I, Williamson GD, Rennie D, Moher D, Becker BJ, Sipe TA, Thacker SB. Meta-analysis of observational studies in epidemiology: a proposal for reporting. Meta-analysis Of Observational Studies in Epidemiology (MOOSE) group. *JAMA.* 2000 Apr 19;283(15):2008-12

Taneja US. E. e-Healthcare in India: critical success factors for sustainable health systems.

Thagard P. Explanatory Coherence. *Behav Brain Scien,* 1989, 12:435-67.

Thorndike EL. A constant error in psychological ratings. J Applied Psychol, 1920, 4:469-77.

Tom SM, Fox CR, Trepel C, Poldrack RA. The neural basis of loss aversion in decision-making under risk. *Science.* 2007 315:515-8

Trepel C, Fox CR, Poldrack RA. Prospect theory on the brain? Toward a cognitive neuroscience of decision under risk. *Brain Res Cogn Brain Res.* 2005 23:34-50.

Tversky A, Kahneman D. The Framing of Decisions and the Psychology of Choice. *Science,* 1981, 208:453-8

Tversky A, Kahneman D. Advances in prospect theory: Cumulative representation of uncertainty. J Risk Uncertainty 1992, 5:297-323.

Viner J. The Utility Concept in Value Theory and Its Critics. J Pol Econ, 1925, 33:369–87.

*Stud Health Technol Inform.* 2007;129:257-61

Vlek C, Skolnik M, Gatersleben B. Sustainable development and quality of life: expected effects of prospective changes in economic and environmental conditions. *Z Exp Psychol.* 1998 45:319-33.

Walter H, Abler B, Ciaramidaro A, Erk S. Motivating forces of human actions. Neuroimaging reward and social interaction. *Brain Res Bull.* 2005 67:368-81.

Whitlock EP, Lin JS, Chou R, Shekelle P, Robinson KA. Using existing systematic reviews in complex systematic reviews. *Ann Intern Med* 2008 148:776-82

Wholey JS. Evaluation: promise and performance. Washington, D.C.: Urban Institute, 1979.

Wholey JS. *Evaluability assessment: developing program theory.* In L. Bickman (Ed.) Using program theory in evaluation. New Directions for Program Evaluation. No. 33. San Francisco: Jossey-Bass, 1987

# ACKNOWLEDGMENTS

This work is dedicated to Olivia, the power of love behind all of my endeavors.

The author is indebted to Drs. Nervina and Maida for the many, deep and friendly discussions about the fundamentals of sustainable evidence-based decision-making – the why, the how, and the teaching of it. The author is also indebted to the colleagues, graduate students and undergraduate students who have actively participated in the elaboration of the theoretical and practical construct of evidence-based research and evidence-based practice elaborated here.

Lastly, the author is indebted to all of the stellar minds who have in the past, who do in the present, and who will in the future guide the human family through the critical steps of change toward a sustainable lifestyle for this and future generations.

# INDEX

## A

abiotic, 55
abusive, 9
academic, 6, 35, 62, 65
accessibility, 54
accountability, 32, 33, 35, 62
accounting, 62
acculturation, 2
accuracy, 6, 54
achievement, 48, 49, 50
acute, 58
ADA, xiii, 21, 65
adaptation, 37, 43, 44, 54, 62
administration, 45
adolescence, 8, 9
adsorption, 46
adult, 51
adulthood, 8, 9
age, 39, 40, 47, 51
agents, 57, 58
aging, 9
agriculture, 43, 44
aid, 55, 58
AIDS, 37, 57, 69
air, 40, 42, 43, 44, 47, 57
algorithm, 70

alternative, xii, 1, 2, 6, 13, 15, 16, 44, 46, 52, 55, 56, 58
alternative energy, 44, 46
Alzheimer's disease, 8, 38
American Association for the Advancement of Science, 65
American Psychiatric Association, 8
amygdala, 7, 8
anaerobic, 46
anaerobic bacteria, 46
analysts, 32
analytical techniques, 5
animal studies, 58
animals, 57, 58
anthropological, 42
application, 6, 31, 33, 57, 68
argument, 6, 10, 17, 34, 35
Aristotelian, 35
arousal, 37
artificial intelligence, 35
asia, 70
assessment, xiii, 6, 12, 24, 28, 30, 44, 46, 50, 52, 53, 57, 58, 59, 73
assessment tools, 57
assumptions, 11, 13, 27
astrocytes, 7
atmosphere, 40, 44

**D**

## O

## N

## P

## T

**Y**